United Nations in the C
World

C000112858

The Making of the Contemporary World
Edited by Eric Evans and Ruth Henig,
both at Lancaster University

The Making of the Contemporary World series provides challenging interpretations of contemporary issues and debates within strongly defined historical frameworks. The range of the series is global, with each volume drawing together material from a range of disciplines – including economics, politics and sociology. The books in this series present compact, indispensable introductions for students studying the modern world. Forthcoming titles include:

Thatcher and Thatcherism
Eric J. Evans

The Soviet Union in World Politics, 1945–1991
G.K. Roberts

The Uniting of Europe
From Discord to Concord
Stanley Henig

The International Economy since 1945
Sidney Pollard

Latin America
John Ward

China under Communism
Alan Lawrence

The Cold War
An interdisciplinary history
David Painter

The Green Movement
Dick Richardson

The Irish Question
Patrick Maume

Decolonization
Raymond Betts

Right Wing Extremism
Paul Hainsworth

United Nations in the Contemporary World

David J. Whittaker

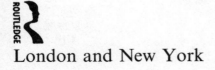

ROUTLEDGE
London and New York

First published 1997
by Routledge
11 New Fetter Lane, London EC4P 4EE

Simultaneously published in the USA and Canada
by Routledge
29 West 35th Street, New York, NY 10001

© 1997 David J. Whittaker
David J. Whittaker has asserted his moral right to be identified as the author of this work in accordance with the Copyright, Designs & Patent Act 1988.

Typeset in Times by
BC Typesetting, Bristol

Printed and bound in Great Britain by
Clays Ltd, St. Ives PLC

All rights reserved. No part of this book may be reprinted or reproduced or utilized in any form or by any electronic, mechanical, or other means, now known or hereafter invented, including photocopying and recording, or in any information storage or retrieval system, without permission in writing from the publishers.

British Library Cataloguing in Publication Data
A catalogue record for this book is available from the British Library

Library of Congress Cataloging-in-Publication Data
Whittaker, David J., 1925–
United Nations in the contemporary world/David J. Whittaker.
p. cm. – (The making of the contemporary world)
Includes bibliographical references and index.
ISBN 0–415–15317–4
1. United Nations. I. Title. II. Series.
JX1977.Z8W48 1997
341.23–dc21 97–2973
CIP

Contents

Preface

A professor once surprised his students by declaring, 'When I ask you questions all I get is answers!' This book on the United Nations sets out to provide a compact introduction to the UN as a powerful actor in the contemporary world. The text presents a number of challenging and argumentative points in the hope of encouraging the reader to ask questions and to go to the many interesting and authoritative discussions of the Organisation, its foundation, its successes and failures. It is hoped that this short introduction will be helpful to students taking modular courses and those able to take advantage of interdisciplinary perspectives.

The book is organised in three parts. Part I consists of three chapters analysing the principles and infrastructure of the UN. Chapter 1 looks at ideas and structures as they were conceived by the founders in 1945. Chapter 2 surveys the extent to which the basic ideas and approaches have changed over the years. Chapter 3 examines the critical issue of how far sovereign states as UN members act in concert. The part played by two of the founding members, the United Kingdom and the United States, is particularly considered. Part II is a series of case studies analysing UN work in the context of the constantly changing international environment. The topics in Chapters 4 to 8 are peacekeeping, arms control and disarmament, the UN and the developing world, the UN and an urbanising world, helping refugees. Each chapter includes pointers to crucial issues which today's UN faces. Part III considers the UN's future. Chapter 9 looks at prospects for UN internal reform, a matter arousing much debate at present. Chapter 10 briefly summarises earlier material and adds a selective list of UN achievements. Other features of this study are a list of UN abbreviations, a guide to further reading and a list of useful addresses and of easily obtainable printed sources.

A book such as this owes a great deal to sharing the thoughts of others in print, conversation and correspondence. I acknowledge with gratitude the support and constructive suggestions of my colleagues in the University of Teesside, especially Dr Carolyn Kitching and Dr Dick Richardson. A number of years of fruitful and affable work with students in the University of Teesside have helped me make sense of my efforts in this book. Lastly, without the indefatigable and careful word processing of Jane Thompson, the resourceful advice of Marianne, my wife, and the encouragement and watchfulness of Heather McCallum and her colleagues at Routledge, this work of mine would never have come alive. For any shortcomings or inaccuracies I am solely responsible.

Abbreviations

ASEAN	Association of South East Asian Nations
CBMs	Confidence Building Measures
CBW	Chemical and Biological Weapons
CSCE	Council for Security and Cooperation in Europe (now OSCE)
CTB	Comprehensive Test Ban
CTBT	Comprehensive Test Ban Treaty
DHA	Department of Humanitarian Affairs
DPs	Displaced Persons
EC	European Community (now European Union)
ECOSOC	Economic and Social Council
FAO	Food and Agriculture Organisation
G7	Group of Seven (main industrial states: USA, UK, Japan, Germany, France, Canada, Italy)
G77	Group of 77 (chiefly developing states)
GATT	General Agreement on Tariffs and Trade
IAEA	International Atomic Energy Authority
IBRD	International Bank for Reconstruction and Development (World Bank)
ICJ	International Court of Justice
IMF	International Monetary Fund
IPC	Integrated Programme for Commodities
IRO	International Refugee Organisation
ITU	International Telecommunications Union
LDCs	Least Developed Countries
MBFR	Mutual Balanced Force Reduction
NATO	North Atlantic Treaty Organisation
NGO	Non-governmental Organisation
NIEO	New International Economic Order
NNWS	Non-nuclear Weapon States

NPT	Non-proliferation Treaty
NWFZ	Nuclear Weapons Free Zone
NWS	Nuclear Weapon States
OAS	Organisation of American States
OAU	Organisation of African Unity
OEOA	Office of Emergency Operations Africa
OPEC	Organisation of Arab Petroleum Exporting Countries
OSCE	Organisation for Security and Cooperation in Europe (previously CSCE)
P5	The Five Security Council Permanent Members (USA, UK, Russia (USSR before December 1991), China, France)
PNET	Peaceful Nuclear Explosions Treaty (1976)
PTBT	Partial Test Ban Treaty (1963)
SEATO	South East Asia Treaty Organisation
TTBT	Threshold Test Ban Treaty (1974)
UK	United Kingdom
UN	United Nations
UNCED	United Nations Conference on Environment and Development (Rio, 1992)
UNCHS	United Nations Centre for Human Settlements
UNCTAD	United Nations Conference on Trade and Development (1983)
UNDP	United Nations Development Programme
UNDRO	United Nations Disaster Relief Organisation
UNEP	United Nations Environment Programme
UNESCO	United Nations Educational, Scientific and Cultural Organisation
UNFICYP	United Nations Peacekeeping Force in Cyprus
UNHCR	United Nations High Commission for Refugees
UNICEF	United Nations Children's Fund
UNIDO	United Nations Industrial Development Organisation
UNITAF	Unified Task Force in Somalia
UNOSOM I	United Nations Operation in Somalia I
UNOSOM II	United Nations Operation in Somalia II
UNPAAERD	United Nations Programme for African Economic Recovery and Development
UNPROFOR	United Nations Protection Force (Bosnia)
UNTAC	United Nations Transitional Authority in Cambodia
UNTEA	United Nations Temporary Executive Authority (West Irian)

UPU	Universal Postal Union
US/USA	United States/United States of America
USSR	Union of Soviet Socialist Republics (before December 1991)
WFP	World Food Programme
WHO	World Health Organisation

By kind permission of Andrzej Krause

Part I
Infrastructural change

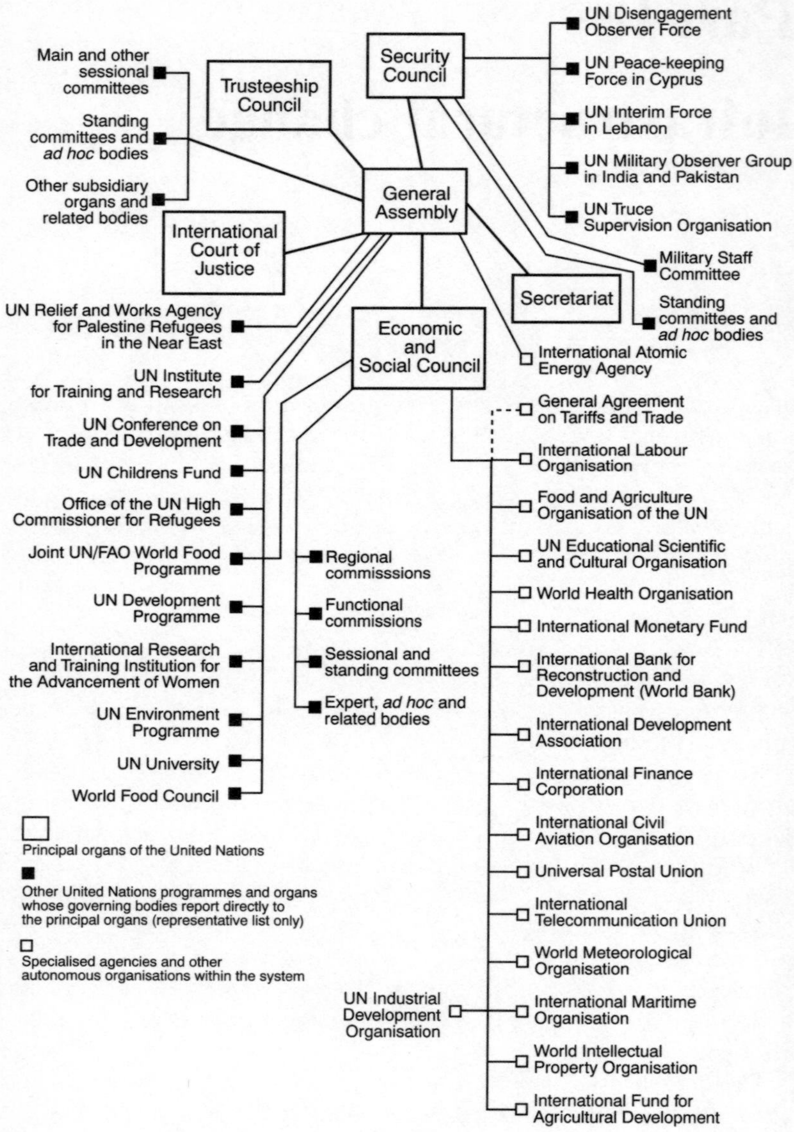
Security Council
Trusteeship Council
General Assembly
International Court of Justice
Secretariat
Economic and Social Council
Main and other sessional committees
Standing committees and ad hoc bodies
Other subsidiary organs and related bodies
UN Disengagement Observer Force
UN Peace-keeping Force in Cyprus
UN Interim Force in Lebanon
UN Military Observer Group in India and Pakistan
UN Truce Supervision Organisation
Military Staff Committee
Standing committees and ad hoc bodies
International Atomic Energy Agency
General Agreement on Tariffs and Trade
International Labour Organisation
Food and Agriculture Organisation of the UN
UN Educational Scientific and Cultural Organisation
World Health Organisation
International Monetary Fund
International Bank for Reconstruction and Development (World Bank)
International Development Association
International Finance Corporation
International Civil Aviation Organisation
Universal Postal Union
International Telecommunication Union
World Meteorological Organisation
International Maritime Organisation
World Intellectual Property Organisation
International Fund for Agricultural Development
UN Industrial Development Organisation
UN Relief and Works Agency for Palestine Refugees in the Near East
UN Institute for Training and Research
UN Conference on Trade and Development
UN Childrens Fund
Office of the UN High Commissioner for Refugees
Joint UN/FAO World Food Programme
UN Development Programme
International Research and Training Institution for the Advancement of Women
UN Environment Programme
UN University
World Food Council
Regional commisssions
Functional commissions
Sessional and standing committees
Expert, ad hoc and related bodies
Principal organs of the United Nations
Other United Nations programmes and organs whose governing bodies report directly to the principal organs (representative list only)
Specialised agencies and other autonomous organisations within the system

The UN system
Source: United Nations Publications

1 The ideas and structures of 1945

In the contemporary world of the 1990s the UN is an important political force. From time to time its efforts and standing are praised; sometimes they are misunderstood and even held in contempt. In order to appraise the UN's significance today it is important to take a look at the infant organisation at the time of its foundation half a century ago. This chapter will briefly survey the UN's purpose, principles and structure as its founders established them. The following chapter will then be able to consider the contemporary position of the UN.

The Second World War altered the shape of international relations visibly and irreversibly. As war drew to a close in 1944–5 the most challenging consequences were to be the waning of Europe's influence (much of the region was prostrate and shattered), the emergence of a US superpower role, the spreading of Soviet and Communist influence, the dawn of a nuclear age (part exciting and part threatening), the growth of bipolar tension and hostility, later to be known as the Cold War, and the beginnings of nationalist agitation in Africa and Asia. Much of Europe was twice devastated – at the preliminary Nazi occupation and subsequently during Allied liberation. There was a vast toll in human lives, half of them civilian, with millions of people uprooted from their homes. Parts of Asia also were in ruins with survivors left forlorn. The task of rehabilitation in country after country was immense.

The hallmarks of feeling among governments and people in 1945 were anguish, hope and determination. Anguish, at six years of carnage wrought by the Axis Powers and at the searing counter-response of the ultimately victorious Allies, was almost overwhelming. There had to be hope that out of the solidarity such as wartime experiences had welded there could be built a postwar world of safety, justice and returning prosperity. Major powers were standing tall in their determination to use their resources and will to lead others in a campaign to reinvigorate civilisation. They had won the war and they would now win the peace. Collaboration, trust, tolerance and international law would replace unilateral selfishness, deceit, violation of human rights and lawlessness.

PRELIMINARY SPADEWORK

Bridgeheads in planning the UN were the Atlantic Charter of 1941 when twenty-six nations supported eight principles for world reconstruction, Allied conferences at Teheran in 1943, and at Yalta and Potsdam in 1945. Much detailed drafting was done in the United States at Dumbarton Oaks in 1944. The shaping of principles and purpose was promoted vigorously by the great Allied leaders, Franklin D. Roosevelt and Winston Churchill. These two, advised by committees and working parties of politicians, soldiers and academics, acknowledged that building a more peaceful world would depend upon consensus and resolve, not all that different from what the Western Powers were relying upon to win the war. Strength of purpose and strength of resources would be keys to survival. There were Anglo-American differences in approach. Churchill was largely governed by a realistic wish to finish the war first. Conscious of old political enmities in Europe and the budding perhaps of new ones, his preference was for an international peacekeeping organisation built out of regional blocs. Britain and its Commonwealth would play a leading part. Roosevelt, equally aware of old geopolitical tensions, went for a more global approach encompassing all continents. The will and power of sovereign states would be spearheaded by the custodial role of Four Policemen (the USA, the UK, the USSR and China) seeking to advance peace and progress by maintaining a vigilance over international developments. This knitting together of idealism, realism and responsibility was to be sounded emphatically by Roosevelt's successor, President Harry Truman, to the opening conference of the UN in San Francisco on 26 June 1945: 'the powerful nations', he said, 'have a duty to assume responsibility for leadership toward a world of peace. . . . By their own example the strong nations of the world should lead the way to international justice.' Nobody could live in peace unless that peace were defended. And no future United States could afford to stand aside in isolation from that duty.

Aside from the public pronouncements of leaders there was a great deal of intensive backroom work going on in the 1940s to launch a new organisation and to bring it into the fitting-out basin. In the beleaguered Britain of 1942 a Foreign Office Economic and Reconstruction Department regularly despatched memos and blueprints to the War Cabinet. In retrospect some of its recommendations echo the optimism of 1919 when an American President, Woodrow Wilson, had championed the idea of a League of Nations to promote peace through a Covenant of humanitarian principles, democratic discussion, openness, arbitration and equality of status for all members. Then, the visionary Wilson had been checked by the Allied victors of the 1914–18 war who called for a higher executive level of major powers with responsibility for enforcing peace. Yet, the League ideals were to fail because those major powers preferred to win peace (as well as war) through negotiating safeguards for their own narrow security. Not surprisingly, covert agreement, sabre-rattling and bluff put an end to early hopes of transparency of intent and accord. Wilson himself became drained of political credibility in an isolationist United States despite his plea that standing by League principles and helping Europe come together to prevent war would in the end avoid the future loss of American lives. After a second world war hard-headed proposals were to guard against any repetition of the mistakes of a previous generation. A close group of Great Powers, winners of war and guarantors of peace, must exercise control of security issues with smaller powers fulfilling a subsidiary role. Realists saw this as working against the dissension and futility that had crippled the League of Nations and had helped to breed cynicism and complacency. Others, more idealist, began to wonder whether the paramountcy of the Big Four was not a conventional system of power politics thinly disguised. (This surmise, as we shall see later, has gained conviction and strength.)

Across the Atlantic, in Washington, teams of advisers were helped by having a President who proved a better listener than his British counterpart. Roosevelt was convinced that the League of Nations had failed because it tried to deal with situations *after* they had become *faits accomplis*. Henceforth there must be anticipatory and unanimous action. More helpfully than in Britain, members of the United States Senate and House of Representatives toured their country from coast to coast airing principles and mobilising public opinion through town meetings and radio talks. It looked as though preliminary spadework was digging deep into fertile soil. People in Europe and in America, chastened by war, were ready to rebuild their world.

Given that there was appreciable unanimity among those working on the rudiments of a new international organisation burning questions were soon being asked as more people were recruited for the drafting process. In the interests of world peace would member states be prepared to give up any of their precious sovereignty? Could the new organisation have sufficient authority to compel members to accept decisions? If Big Power leadership was said to be vital to secure world peace would smaller nations be ready to go along with that? If the strength of a state's autonomy were acknowledged would this reinforce collective potential or would it weaken it?

The UN Charter, coming off the drawing board, was mainly an Anglo-American product. Western liberal principles were prominently there as they had been in the Covenant of the League of Nations a generation earlier. The definitive version was assembled over sixty-two days by national representatives and 'consultants' from forty-two non-governmental organisations (NGOs), working all hours in Californian heat. Fifty-one states, representing four-fifths of the world's population in those days, came to San Francisco to sign the document on 26 June 1945 and it was finally ratified by those signatories on 24 October, a day ever since known as 'UN Day'.

THE PURPOSE OF THE UN

Article 1 of the UN Charter enumerates the basic purposes of the UN. In brief, they are to maintain international peace and security, to develop friendly relations among nations, to achieve international cooperation in solving problems, and to act as a centre for harmonising collective action. These purposes are action loaded. They only bear fruit if 'collective measures' are appropriate and effective. The UN is to serve three interrelated functions: namely, to be a forum for discussion and decision, to meet as a syndicate for action, employing non-forcible measures to improve the world, and to be a missionary centre appealing to moral values and standards higher than those generally prevailing in international relations.

PRINCIPLES IN THE UN CHARTER

The authors of the UN Charter certainly recognised that the earlier principles of the League of Nations were neither fully nor consistently observed. This time the new organisation would empower principles. The most important ones are set out below.

The association principle

The fifty-one signatories at San Francisco were to be joined by all other peace-loving states accepting Charter obligations. Each would respect the sovereign equality of all other members. They would never resort to force in settling disputes. They must rally to the assistance of the UN whenever required. Any violation of Charter principles could lead to expulsion.

The hierarchy principle

A General Assembly as the bottom tier would offer all member states a forum for discussion and recommendation. International collaboration in the widest possible field of international relations would be promoted. Executive functions would be the remit of a Security Council, an upper tier, with primary responsibility for maintenance of peace and security and for the regulation of armaments and for dealing effectively with disputes and threats to the peace. Restorative action, so far as possible, would not involve the use of force although 'appropriate measures' might ultimately be considered necessary. A Military Staff Committee and standby enforcement contingents were to be provided for. Matters other than procedural would observe a principle of unanimity. In the event of the Security Council having a dispute or situation under consideration the General Assembly must refrain from making any recommendations unless invited to do so.

The principle of collective security

This was implicit in many of the principles rather than the subject of explicit ruling. Generally, members would take 'effective collective measures' for the prevention and removal of threats to the peace and for the suppression of aggressive acts and breaches of the peace. They were to work for the 'adjustment or settlement' of threatening disputes or situations. The Charter allocated this call to action to the province of the executive Security Council and not to the deliberative General Assembly, but the obligation of rallying to the cause was clear enough. Two chapters, Chapters VI and VII, outline procedures to be followed, for dispute reconciliation and the contingency of more forceful measures. There were two important riders to this principle. First, nothing in the Charter authorised the UN to intervene in matters essentially within the domestic jurisdiction of any state or, indeed, required it to submit such matters for settlement

(Article 2.7). Further, nothing in the Charter was to impair the inherent right of individual or collective self-defence if one member were to attack another. This was understood as an interim measure at least until the Security Council could intervene (Article 51).

The regional principle

Yet another principle seems at odds with the universalist intentions of an instrument for collective security. Nothing in the Charter was to preclude the existence of regional arrangements or agencies for dealing with peace maintenance provided their way of working was consistent with UN purposes and principles. These regional bodies might even be used for enforcement action but only if the Security Council authorised it.

The mediation principle

Peacekeeping, later to become a major UN enterprise, is not mentioned as the implementation of a principle. In the general context of members' obligation to settle disputes peacefully and to refrain from using force there is an entire chapter, Chapter VI, suggesting ways of talking through solutions. In the event of deadlock the Security Council and possibly an International Court of Justice should work to freeze or contain a dispute which might become a crisis or conflict.

The trusteeship principle

The UN was born at a time of transition and turmoil among perhaps 700 million people either yoked to empires or given nominal autonomy as League of Nations mandated territories. Three chapters in the Charter trace the UN's concern, by way of a Declaration, to carry out a 'sacred trust' to promote the well-being and advance of these people. In principle, an International Trusteeship System and a Trusteeship Council would have this responsibility.

The judicial principle

Conformity with the principles of international law was to be a cardinal principle for the UN as it had been for the former League of Nations. Following on the nineteen chapters of the UN Charter is the Statute of an International Court of Justice. A preliminary chapter in the Charter signals the importance of such a court and the Statute goes on to establish in great detail the Court's organisation, competence and procedures.

The economic and social principle

Two whole chapters, Chapters IX and X, address the principle of taking on board 'all international economic, social, cultural, education, health and related matters'. This would be the task of an Economic and Social Council overseeing an array of specialised agencies. In particular, such a council would be expected to promote respect for, and observance of, human rights and fundamental freedoms for all.

THE UN'S ORIGINAL STRUCTURE

With the Charter printed, signed and ratified the next step in the autumn of 1945 was to breathe life into a structure to implement purpose and principles. Some of the outline principles had already been threaded into structural schemes, among them those relating to collective security, trusteeship, economic and social promotion, and jurisdiction. A UN Preparatory Commission, split into ten working parties, worked in London during the winter months to establish procedural rules, modalities of voting, procedures for assemblies and committees, and the preparation of preliminary agendas. League of Nations principles and ways of working were examined closely for the sake of continuity. As might be expected there was some fear of arousing latent hostilities or creating doubts by reason of the League's chequered history. In the end, it was decided to locate the UN in the newer world of the Americas, in New York, rather than in Geneva. Roosevelt, already in February 1945, had his mind made up about this: 'Not Geneva. Geneva's unlucky, has an unlucky record . . .'.

Structural elements of the UN were hoisted into place in a rudimentary form in late 1945. At the outset today's six main components of the UN were there in embryo – the General Assembly, the Security Council, the Secretariat, the Economic and Social Council, the Trusteeship Council and the International Court of Justice.

THE GENERAL ASSEMBLY

Each member state was entitled to seat up to five delegates. Regardless of size, each state could have only one vote. The Assembly was no legislating parliament. As a meeting house it was to rely on debate in plenary sessions each autumn and sometimes in Special Sessions. Delegates would meet to adopt resolutions, and Declarations, to encourage their governments to implement these, and to put their whole weight behind any ratified Convention for that would be a mandatory instrument. Committees would commission surveys, consider reports, establish working groups, and frame programmes.

THE SECURITY COUNCIL

Five permanent members (the USA, the UK, the USSR, China, France) and ten non-permanent members would meet continuously as an executive arm. Prevention and conciliation were to be their approach to maintaining peace and security and they would seek to work forward from common ground rather than from short-term national preoccupations. There would be no progress without the affirmative votes of all permanent members.

THE SECRETARIAT

Administratively the first task was to enlist staff to set up provisional working arrangements. Paramount considerations were to be the highest standards of efficiency, competence and integrity with due regard to the importance of recruiting staff on as wide a geographical basis as possible. Fourteen thousand people from a score of countries were eventually appointed. Their loyalty had to be to the UN and to nobody else. A Secretary-General would head the Secretariat. Apart from day-to-day administrative activities the Secretary-General was to chair meetings and report to the General Assembly on UN activities each year. Serving a five-year term the Secretary-General could be re-elected for a second term. At the pinnacle of UN responsibility the Secretary-General would be a critical figure in contemporary world politics, an organiser on a grand scale, an influential reformer, an initiator who might bring to the attention of the Security Council any matter which might threaten the maintenance of international peace and security.

THE ECONOMIC AND SOCIAL COUNCIL

This body was to be the coordinating group for most UN activities apart from the maintenance of peace and security. (Later to be known as ECOSOC there would be impressive growth here in size and breadth of operation.) Essentially, the first task of this arm of the UN would be to put in hand the mammoth task of reconstruction and resettlement in war-torn regions. It was envisaged that smaller nations would play an important part in a forum of fifty-four state representatives who would formulate policy recommendations, commission research and reports, and convene conferences. Liaison was to be maintained with representatives of governments, with expert advisers, and with research institutes.

Specialised agencies were to be established by intergovernment agreement as separate, independent entities with distinctive mandates and methods of working yet maintaining close links with the UN. This ambitious structure owes much to the prewar principle of 'functionalism' as it was enunciated by the sociologist, David Mitrany, working in the United States. His thinking was that collaboration among nations would put an end to *laissez-faire* and parochialism and would promote better living conditions for the world's peoples and might encourage and bring about cooperation in the more difficult political arena. Success in the one might 'spill over' and 'ramify' to bring further success elsewhere. Thinking such as this appealed to the founders of the UN in the late 1940s. Might not irrationality and conflict give way before rational policy sharing and realistic ways of working? Nations united realistically on the ground, as it were, could pragmatically work towards idealistic goals. Specialised agencies (as the name suggests) would be given specific, specialised roles. In 1945 ECOSOC took into the UN fold two existing intergovernmental bodies of venerable age. They were UPU and ITU, both working in postal and communications services since 1874 and 1875. Eventually, there were to be eighteen or so agencies. They work more as a network than a system, initiating programmes and sharing projects in a vast array of enterprises – health, food and agriculture, labour affairs, trade, refugees, international finance, education, meteorology, air and sea transport. Known to the world by their acronyms (see the list of abbreviations) like WHO, FAO, ILO, UNHCR, UNESCO, IBRD, they have headquarters in Geneva, Rome, Paris, Vienna and Nairobi. At the outset in 1945 the responsibility of each agency would be to transmit data from enquiry, inventories, research and field trials back to ECOSOC so that the General Assembly could use the information to put into codes, guidelines and covenants. Mitrany's notion that peace would come about 'in pieces' would surely mean the work of agencies putting meaning into the premise of the UN Charter (as UNESCO proclaimed it) that 'since wars begin in the minds of men it is in the minds of men that the defences of peace must be constructed'.

THE TRUSTEESHIP COUNCIL

This council would exercise a general supervision of 'trust territories' to be groomed for self-government or complete independence (eleven of them) and of 'non-trust territories' (seventy-two of them) where a lesser degree of autonomy from former colonial powers was to be expected. The Council would compile reports, pay inspection visits, and accept petitions from territorial groups. There would be close liaison with ECOSOC. Very clearly, the UN would take this duty most seriously and there would be an end to the rather limp and not very productive mandatory and protectorate regimes of the old League of Nations.

THE INTERNATIONAL COURT OF JUSTICE

Here the Court's Statute was adopted at the same time as the UN Charter but it was to take two years before the Court commenced its work. Basically, this court was seen as an institution to develop and refine the process of international law through rulings on what were termed 'justiciable cases' where parties await judgment. There was an expectation that litigants would abide by the Court's judgment but there was no power of arrest, punishment or enforcement. Indeed, the Charter acknowledged that UN members might go to other tribunals to resolve their differences. The compilers of both Charter and Statute certainly had in mind the usefulness of asking a court to give advisory opinions, for instance as to the interpretation of a treaty, the extent of reparations following legal violations or the obligations of states in regard to regulations and quotas, or nationality and immigration matters.

THE FIRST GENERAL ASSEMBLY

A long drawn-out midwifery process, cosmopolitan and often vociferous, had brought a robust infant into the daylight by January 1946. 'Austerity' London worked hard to clean up its Central Hall in war-damaged Westminster for the official inauguration of a working UN. To be holding it there was conceived as tribute to a resolute Britain. Gladwyn Jebb (later Lord Gladwyn), of the British Foreign Office, was to be the UN's Acting Secretary-General. With British and American colleagues he had helped draft the blueprints of the UN during the war. (He was to be succeeded on 1 February 1946 by the Norwegian, Trygve Lie.) Two thousand delegates from all over the world met beneath the new blue and gold flag of the UN as delegates to the UN's first General Assembly. Some of them considered it significant and auspicious that the occasion provided seating not only for formally attired-and-labelled government representatives but also for eager participants from some 800 bona fide observer groups (the NGOs as they were later to be termed). The unity of nations had got under way with something of a democratic flavour. Yet within six months, as the next chapter relates, there was speculation in some quarters as to the future. How would the UN's purpose, principles and structure respond when subjected to the divisive tensions of a polarising world?

2 Changing UN ideas and approaches

In the year 2000 the UN will be 55 years old. This chapter will hold a mirror to the expectations of the UN's founders of 1945 in an attempt to discover how Charter principles may have changed since then. Principles examined will again be those to do with association, hierarchy, collective security, regionalism, mediation, trusteeship, the judicial principles of international law, and economic and social principles. Finally, there will be a brief consideration of how the UN has attempted from time to time to translate some of these principles into action plans.

PRINCIPLES

The association principle

The admission of all peace-loving states which accepted Charter obligations was clear enough in regard to the states gathered at the opening conference in San Francisco. Mistrust arose, as might be expected, over former enemies like Germany and Japan. There were, after all, two Germanies. It was not until 1973 that the UN accepted membership of the Federal Republic of Germany (West Germany) and of the German Democratic Republic (East Germany). Italy was allowed in in 1955 and Japan in 1956. The main contretemps arose over those states considered to be in Capitalist or Socialist ranks, blocs increasingly arranged in stern opposition. During the years 1946 to 1961 the USSR blackballed admission of a number of Western candidates (Ceylon, Ireland, Italy, Jordan, Portugal and Spain) casting ninety-six vetoes to do so. This was in reprisal for Western reluctance over certain East European states (Albania, Bulgaria, Hungary and Romania). Eventually, both sides relented in 1955 when all these aspiring members were admitted in a 'package deal'. The United States would not countenance either Vietnam or Angola joining until 1976 and 1977. A rump clique in Taiwan was seen as the representative of China (largely Communist then) until 1971. Argument and counter-claim were aired fiercely in the first few years. To the strident charge that the UN Charter was a Western creation heavy with non-Socialist ethos there was the reply that the Charter and the very shape of the new institution was underpinned by a variety of cultures, creeds and political beliefs. Surely it was a web of political responses that clouded straightforward acceptance? The only thing that Afghanistan, Iceland, Yemen and Thailand proclaimed in common was a feeling of sincere and objective loyalty to the Big Idea of universalism restoring civilisation.

General Assembly members for the best part of the first thirty years of the UN could be seen as belonging to three fairly distinct groups. The Premier League of players were those five permanent members of the Security Council whom we have met already as initiators, prime founders and determined guarantors. The Second League players were the independent minded such as Brazil, Japan, Italy, Australia, Poland, Finland, Norway and the Netherlands. Weak in isolation they were robust in principled concert. They were loyal, innovative, active in amplifying public awareness of the usefulness of the UN. They were active in nudging the permanent members into consistent attitudes and decisions. Third, and largely after 1961, there emerged the so-called 'non-aligned' group. Sometimes regarded as blatantly anti-Western in their early days and as rigidly ideological, their common concern was to cut away from the implacable opposed fronts of the superpowers as the Cold War froze positive advance. They were hostile to the colonialism of Britain, France, the Netherlands and Portugal. Anxious to take the stage in associated advance, calling for a more representative Security Council, and led by India, Yugoslavia, Indonesia and Nigeria, they acquired political salience and eventually, topping the hundred mark, constituted some two-thirds of UN membership.

Apart from the divisive effect of the Cold War there has emerged the question of what one might term states-centrism. Are the 'peoples of the United Nations', so hopefully referred to in the Charter's Prologue, to be represented only by states that for many are pawns in a rather obsolescent *status quo*? Might groups other than states legitimately and effectively act as a popular assembly? Debate apart, there is no sign of sovereign states losing their confident places at the UN. After all, a former Prime Minister of Israel, Mrs Golda Meir, had assured the world community that 'internationalism does not mean the end of individual nations. Orchestras don't mean the end of violins.' Yet the principle of association is set about with questions of legitimacy. If a state takes on the nature of a dictatorial regime is there not a conflict between that other principle of sovereign integrity and the right of individuals, perhaps of a large group, to exercise the right of self-determination and basic freedom? While the world is becoming more interdependent (in a fashion that would have pleased those of 1945) the encouragement of self-determination is leading to secession, rivalry and turmoil. Apart from macro-nationalism, which was not always conducive to peaceful association, we now have micro-nationalism. Boutros Boutros-Ghali, when he was UN Secretary-General, spoke of this challenge in these terms: 'Nations are too interdependent, national frontiers are too porous and transnational realities – in the sphere of technology and investment, on the one side, and poverty and misery on the other – are too dangerous to permit egocentric isolationism.' Today there is a wave of new states crowding into the UN's association – Armenia, Azerbaijan, Georgia, Tajikistan and others, parts of the old USSR exercising concepts of freedom, unity and independent voice. With the meltdown of the Cold War antagonisms there is little to hold in check antipathies that are ethnic, linguistic or religious. The elegant quadrille of the diplomats has become the helter-skelter of assertive groups the world over. Must the principle of states-in-association be reviewed?

The hierarchy principle

There has been structural expansion and modification. Basic functions of the General Assembly forum and of the executive Security Council are still separable. The contemporary forum is a different throng of 185 delegates rather than fifty. In the three months they meet in full session they pass twice as many resolutions as did their predecessors but this reflects the increasing complexity of a varied agenda whether this ranges over development issues, arms control, or economic and social problems. Decolonisation matters have almost vanished. The first ten years of the UN's existence have been labelled by Evan Luard, its foremost historian, as the Years of Western Domination. The distrust and hostility of those days made it a platform for the self-righteous and a cockpit for protagonists. Idealists were eager to resolve and declaim, realists were sure that political gaming would win the day. The confident words of the Charter about the handling of peace and security were negated amid a fierce battle for hearts and minds. First hopes turned into disillusion as problems basic to wider peace and security, for instance the postwar treaties, German reunification and arms control, Austria, all were not solved but were either sidelined or decided covertly by 'interested' Great Powers. Public discussion frequently took the form of turning a hostile spotlight onto opponents rather than a mutual search for understanding. The mirror into which the UN's founders looked had frosted over. Compromise was surrender.

In the General Assembly, perhaps unavoidably, policy decisions have often been spasmodically framed in improvised slogan form. These are not the detailed considerations which sovereign governments must have to implement proposals. The lower floor of the hierarchy has always begged the question of whether any real diplomacy can be done in a circus ring or a glasshouse. 'It was', thought the Canadian Foreign Minister Lester Pearson, 'the place where we can meet either to settle problems or make settlement more difficult.' Nevertheless, much 'quiet diplomacy' goes on in corridors and meeting lounges. Everything under the sun is, in any case, discussed in seven committees. A wealth of evidence is read by these committees; experts in every field are consulted. While most of this activity goes on unobserved by the public from time to time a topic is given full-scale prominence by being the main theme of a decade, for instance to highlight the problems of women's equality, of racism, of development or the great primary health care campaign of the WHO – Health for All by the Year 2000. From time to time there will be a Special Session, an exercise in 'summitry' to mark the importance of disarmament, food, human rights, population growth, environmental degradation.

If the lower layer of the UN hierarchy has grown and diversified beyond original expectations it is the upper layer which has made progress in fits and starts. In accordance with the Charter the Security Council functions rather like a fuse. The use of the veto, that is to say the dropping of an issue from the agenda because not all the permanent members affirm agreement, has enabled the superpowers to ensure that their cardinal interests are protected. Equally, the device has prevented any one power from dominating proceedings. This double bind illustrated by the intransigence of the UK and France over Suez in 1956, the stern 'keep-away' tactics of the USSR over Afghanistan in 1980 and the petulance of the United States over Grenada in 1983 may have helped firm up a position for those who saw themselves in the right. The manoeuvre aroused, though, both discord and disapproving response. In the second place, there is something of a safeguard against arbitrary monopoly. Even if all the permanent members concur no decision is possible without the added agreement of two non-permanent members. It is in regard to the action that the Security Council has been able to take that most controversy is apparent. Chapter VII, in the case of impasse, requires the Security Council to determine the existence of threats or aggressive acts and then either to make recommendations of a pacific nature or to authorise a course of action. This clear determination has led to explicit action in the case of Palestine in 1948, Korea in 1950, Rhodesia in the 1960s and 1970s, over the Falklands in 1982, and in the instance of Iraq in 1987 and 1992. In two of these scenarios (Korea in 1950 and the Gulf in 1992) an active military force was deployed by the United States, acting as it were under franchise to the UN. It is the process of 'determination' that has given the Council a good deal of trouble. Identifying and locating aggression is rarely a matter of detecting a cross-border incursion. All too often it is preceded by much less explicit 'propaganda warfare' which it is difficult for any external agency to reduce or remove. Many so-called examples of aggressive acts have been due to insurgency within a country either against a government or between rivals for power. Undoubtedly, in Charter terms, there were threats to peace and security, but what took place in Cyprus, Kashmir, Malaysia, Goa, Yemen, Lebanon and in Central America was notoriously difficult to figure out and contain. Predictably, the Security Council has come up against the protectionist fence of 'domestic jurisdiction' (Article 2.7).

Given the intensity of feelings behind most disputes and the complexity of the factors involved it is understandable that an organisation lacks the leverage to ensure a long-term and deep-scale reconciliation of issues. There are, however, points of light in years of gloom. The Security Council has become less and less fractured as the millennium approaches. The permanent members are putting their minds and their resources behind peacekeeping missions. Consensus on most issues has replaced contention and station keeping. There is a shift from expediency and peace-at-any-price to heightened awareness, to enlisting experts and consultative groups, to making use of personal contacts that have more meaning and usefulness than the photo-ops so many summits bring in train.

The collective security principle

This principle is possibly the one that has changed most. It has expanded in its meaning; in so many ways it has proved both passive and questionable. One can credit those who wrote the Charter with enough realism (born of the failing experience of the League of Nations) to acknowledge that safety could not be assured without guarantee. The Charter was unlikely in that event to state the need of security either as an abstract thing or as something easily obtained. Members of the new organisation had the obligation to make the world as safe as they could.

In fact, during the Cold War, it seemed as though collective security could only be gained if the UN was indeed passive. Otherwise, a move by way of censure or contemplated intervention might offend the sensibilities of major nuclear powers. In the event, Soviet forces marched into Prague in 1948 and again in 1967, and into Budapest in 1956 with impunity incurring only condemnation by others. At other times, the world held its breath when East and West faced each other over Berlin in 1948–9 and 1958–61. Europe's collective security depended then upon a pull-back from the brink by major contestants without any prospect of UN mediation. It was not long before the terms such as 'peace' and 'security' were connected inseparably. Theoretically, the UN when it came upon a dispute or threat to peace and security would be an impartial third party with a quasi-legal status and a universally accepted regime. Of course disputants would very likely play to the gallery in the UN forum seeking support and claiming legitimation. Despite this the UN, in the words of the Charter, was to 'recommend appropriate procedures or methods of adjustment'.

Whenever possible, 'adjustment' was to follow the route of patient negotiation, pacific 'intervention' in its fullest sense. This has been the way of UN peacekeeping (as we shall see in Chapter 4) save that on occasion the Security Council has authorised an enforcement mission as in Korea and the Gulf. The result in both cases was the attainment of some degree of regional security though in Korea it was a demilitarised stand-off between irreconcilable parties. It is not difficult to imagine how vague and far-reaching expectations about collective security were in the dark days of major power quarrels. Even when there was some sort of accord between members there has generally been confusion as to distinguishing terms the Charter employs like 'dispute' and 'situation'. Fifty years ago disputes were often considered to be disagreements between sovereign states where the issues at stake were visible. Increasingly, international disputes have been many-rooted, temporary collisions or long-standing, simmering resentments flaring into violence. In all cases they appear to be hazardous situations. Things may deteriorate, 'boil over', so that a 'crisis' results spilling over easily onto neighbouring terrain. In the interlocked international relations of the contemporary world any crisis becomes everybody's crisis. How best may an international organisation intervene thousands of miles away from a flash-point? Again, in the perspectives of 1945 the essence of crisis abatement was resourceful and preventive diplomacy, ideally at the behest of aggrieved parties. US research has estimated that since 1945 the UN has been involved in rather more than half of all international crises yet only one in three of these situations yielded a satisfactory outcome. This appears to be a low success rate in view of the dangers of escalation. Likely factors here would seem to be a reluctance among UN members to underpin security with a collective impetus. What should be everybody's business turns out to be nobody's business in particular. That fine principle of 'all for one and one for all' has been fragmented and localised. *Ad hoc* intervention is the first and the last resort. On account of this at least the UN has often been made a scapegoat for confused inaction. It is good to know that in the last five years or so there has been set in motion a very thorough and practicable set of proposals for much more effective and sustained peacekeeping and conflict resolution. This is a programmed approach with wide and long-term objectives for lasting settlement and security incorporating control of factors as varied as possession of weapons, land reform, famine relief, primary health care, provision of water and sanitation. The aim is to address security individually and collectively. Even so, difficult questions dog the principle of security. Tensions nearest to a point of potential conflict may be alleviated but does that ensure safety above all for the people who live there? Can collective security be imposed and in that case does the UN exceed its authority as impartial conciliator? Has security any real meaning if it is impermanent and imprecise?

The regional principle

Acknowledged in the Charter as a useful ancillary to maintaining peace and security, this principle is one that has been subscribed to on many occasions and in many places, in the main as a defensive bulwark. There are no clear guidelines in UN statements in the Charter as to the meaning of the rider that there must be a consistency with the purposes and principles of the UN. A form of first-line defence and a means of deterrence were behind the creation of NATO in 1947, of the Warsaw Pact six years later, of the South East Asia Treaty Organisation (SEATO) in 1954. The Arab League in 1945 and the Inter-American Treaty of Reciprocal Assistance (the Rio Pact of

1947) were part cultural and part rallying to the colours. In the last twenty years European security has been the concern of no less than fifty-two regional politicians in Europe who have come together as the Organisation (now Council) for Security and Cooperation in Europe giving the transnational ideal of collective security lip-service, it has been suggested, while they manoeuvre in much tighter terms. At all meetings of these diverse groupings the UN is seated as an observer.

The mediation principle

Mediation is at the centre of the UN ethos. Arrayed in Article 33 of the UN Charter are techniques for seeking a settlement of disputes. Negotiation, enquiry, conciliation, arbitration, judicial settlement or resort to regional arrangements are the means suggested. Again, US research points to a less than satisfactory performance by the UN. Not quite half of the attempted mediations had a positive outcome; the other half ended either in tacit or unreliable agreement or in no accommodation at all. Intervention by the Security Council has proved more resolute than that of the less formal General Assembly, but even active, well-informed mediation has failed to resolve situations moving into conflict, for example over the partition of Palestine in 1947, in Korea in 1950–3, over Hungary in 1956 and Rhodesia in 1965. Talking issues through in the General Assembly may have failed to secure agreement but at least there is a channel there for debate and for cooling inflamed viewpoints. UN action has often taken the form of low-level resolution through fact finding, the exercise of 'good offices', or the despatch of a Special Representative of the Secretary-General. In Cyprus, Namibia, the Middle East and Cambodia, emissaries of the Secretary-General have worked imaginatively to bring some reconciliation to rival groups. Peacekeeping along these lines in the Middle East has taken for four decades the form of an unremitting and unrewarding watch over events and possible violations of agreements and a cease-fire. The transition to self-determination and a peaceful existence is a long drawn-out process taking thirteen years in Cambodia and twenty years in Namibia. In the one case there was appalling internal strife, in the other the hold of an occupying South Africa had to be prised away through negotiations by the UN and, separately, through the mediation of the United States. As we shall see in Chapter 4 the mediatory principle when translated operationally into the deployment of a *peacekeeping* force only opens a window of opportunity slightly. What must follow if mediation is to effect any long-term solution is a *peace-making* programme for the UN, a process of reconstruction far more comprehensive and costly than anything envisaged back in 1945.

The trusteeship principle

At the inception of the Charter in 1945 this was an expression of a strongly felt obligation, indeed, a 'sacred trust' to promote 'well-being' to the utmost extent. This was always likely to arouse problems in view of the equally strong desire of colonial powers not to relinquish dependence links and useful resources. At the outset eleven trust territories were designated together with seventy-two non-self-governing territories. Fundamentally, the UN's task was to encourage the development of free political institutions and to protect people against discrimination and abuse. Colonial powers were required to lift the yoke of 'alien subjugation, domination and exploitation'. What has followed is a heartening story of success, achieved almost entirely without internal strife. Only one trust territory remains and that is the strategic area of Micronesia in the Pacific administered under international agreement by the United States. Fewer than twenty of the non-self-governing communities are still languishing in dependence and overall eighty nations comprising more than 700 million people have now joined the UN as full members. Newly enfranchised nations fought strenuously for their less fortunate brothers. The General Assembly became an arena for fierce championing of the need to 'liberate' those many millions still held down in subjection. Inevitably, as a majority of UN members were, in fact, direct representatives of newly freed people, the Assembly and the Security Council were pressured into condemning exploitation and racism by colonial powers like Britain, the Netherlands, Belgium, France, Portugal or that of foreign commercial interests. South Africa was vociferously castigated for its policy of apartheid and by 1970 most trading, cultural and sporting links with South Africa had been suspended. Inevitably, the UN itself went beyond condemnation to stand for a process of 'liberation'. There were many difficult questions to face. What could the UN do if a rogue regime like South Africa retreated behind the exclusion clause of the Charter article forbidding UN intervention in matters held to be within domestic jurisdiction? Did condemnation of racial discrimination risk heightening an offender's unwillingness to conform and improve a situation? If the UN goes on to impose sanctions on an errant state how is it possible to ensure that innocent people are not gravely inconvenienced and hurt? How does the UN deal with 'sanctions busting' as happened over Rhodesia and South Africa? What is the position, morally and practically, if an internal resistance movement resorts to violence? And should the UN not reach beyond punitive measures to encourage a process of dialogue and negotiation?

A very basic problem confronts groups which work for liberation in its fullest sense. Attaining self-determination represents repossession, restoration and fuller access to land, resources and opportunity. Liberation must be more than release from what was unequal and denied. In the case of post-apartheid South Africa a rehabilitation programme has to take one in three Africans out of present poverty into a sustainable future. Cambodians now have a measure of relief from violence but they have inherited 100 per cent inflation and only 3 per cent of their water is drinkable. Independence, security and survival are indissolubly linked for trustees.

The judicial principle

This is at the very heart of the purpose of the UN to give substance and life to international law. While this was a matter of conviction among those who designed the UN Charter in 1945 it was unlikely that they regarded an international court of justice as something that nations would enthusiastically resort to. Yet, experience over half a century has demonstrated that the International Court of Justice has a recognised usefulness as a centre for advice and consultation. Detailed examination and interpretation of such complicated matters as the law of the sea, rights of asylum, the duties of mandatory powers, disputes over trading contracts, trade embargoes, complaints about pollution and exploitation of natural resources have all been scrupulously looked at and reported on. This is a modest performance but it is indispensable. It is in the more contentious world of the courtroom itself that difficulties have arisen. Two hundred cases have been brought before the Court's judges in fifty years. This is a bare fraction of the cases that might have been brought had many nations been willing to accept compulsory jurisdiction which might go against them. Perhaps not far from the truth is the cynical observation that international law represents something that even the righteous are unwilling to recognise and that the wicked do not obey. Nevertheless, in the absence of some system of international law the world society of states would fail to enjoy the benefits of trade and commerce, of exchange of ideas, and of normal routine communication. Denied the instruments of arrest and mandatory sentencing the UN's legal institution functions today more as a helping centre and point of reference in an uncertain and inconsistent world.

The economic and social principle

An early emphasis in UN work was that of promoting progress in developing countries where two-thirds of people live. Most of the UN's money and workforce is caught up in schemes for betterment and advance. ECOSOC, as we have seen earlier, was set up to coordinate the work of the central organisation and specialised agencies. Beginning in 1960 the General Assembly went on to establish the mission of ECOSOC through three successive Development Decades. There must be a unified approach to concrete programmes, a move to a new international order 'based on equity, sovereign interdependence, common interest among states irrespective of their economic and social systems which would correct inequalities and redress existing injustices, and make it possible to eliminate the widening gap between developing and developed countries'. This is a laudable and breathtaking perspective. To ensure steadily accelerating economic and social development and to effect this in harness is a tremendous undertaking. Much that is done is menaced by the indebtedness, population explosion and lack of security of developing lands. Security as a concept was only hazily understood in 1945 and then generally in political terms. Today's world demonstrates that security as a state of dependable well-being is not conferred; it has to be worked for in everyday situations.

Another indisputable fact is that everyone suffers from insecurity in whatever sense that word is used. Developing and developed states are locked into a mutuality which puts those who think they are strong and those who know they are weak into a pattern of vulnerability. Hence, the thrust of much UN economic and social programming is 'a battle for better balance'. The desirable objectives of correction, redress, ensuring, elimination are only likely to be approached through appraisal of resources, definition of targets, marshalling of funds and other resources, survey and audit. More than 1945 could ever understand (at least it took them until 1972 to realise it), there must be limits to growth. The UN Charter proclaimed an 'inalienable right to growth'. Does this mean that member states can be encouraged to grow exponentially? A UN Charter of Economic Rights and Duties set a game plan in 1974 cautiously stressing that to exercise a duty would involve restraint. It has not been easy to urge restraint upon young states emerging from years of grudging dependence and lack of material progress. More can readily lead to worse. Measures that are designed to alleviate a problem such as inadequate food supply may bring unfortunate consequences. Do we increase food supplies? The population then grows faster. Is redistribution of incomes to be engineered? Rising gross national products and incomes will lead to faster depletion of natural resources, widen the gap between rich and disadvantaged, and no doubt hasten the ill-effects of waste and pollution. What seems obvious in theory yet difficult to realise in practice is that growth must be sustainable so as not to jeopardise the life chances of future generations. It is in this field that moral, political, economic, sociological and ecological proposals have merged. More must mean better – for all. Development programmes have to have 'a human face' and an affordable set of priorities. These are points to which we will return in Chapter 6.

No corner of the earth is hidden from the eye of the satellite. This ought to reinforce an ability to see problems and issues globally. Ironically, as more than one Secretary-General has pointed out, the common interest in living together securely has tended to assert itself only at times of actual dangerous crisis. Until that point short-term national interests and opportunism override common concern. Is not, though, the contemporary world frequently in a state of interconnected crises? When Adlai Stevenson, a staunch UN supporter, coined the epigram 'eggheads of the world unite: you have nothing to lose but your yolks', he was inferring that only thoughtful and principled and collective action would remove the constraints which hamper positive advance.

FROM PRINCIPLES TO ACTION PLANS

In recent years the efforts of the UN have illustrated principle-in-action in three dramatic ways. First, there have been widening terms of reference in the concepts of 'peace', 'participation', 'development' and security. The three are interlinked. Peace, always more than simply the absence of war, thrives when well-fed, well-housed, literate people maintain a democratic community with vigour, vigilance and unity. Participation is most willing and effective if there is a grassroots, bottom-up convergence on improving present circumstances and ensuring a reasonable future. Development fundamentally is a movement, both qualitative and quantitative, towards defined objectives seen as appropriate and attainable. Security, in the sense of 'fervent hope, sanguine expectation' (as the dictionary puts it), has much to do with how an individual and a group view their material prospects with equanimity. In the second place, tasks have been appraised in global terms to frame up world plans of action and forward-looking strategies. The 6,000 projects of the UN Development Programme (UNDP), sponsored by 150 countries, managed by sixteen specialised agencies and with 8,000 international experts in the field, are a global scheme to rehabilitate people who could never rely upon peace, well-ordered participation, planned progress or reliable expectations. Ambitious UN action plans, often running for five years at a time, are at work in the fields of environmental conservation, population policies, the control of drugs and of AIDS. There are forward-looking strategies for the Advancement of Women to the Year 2000. Third, there is a concern to address issues in the field, to home in on particular needs in specific places. Regionally, the UN Programme for African Economic Recovery and Development (UNPAAERD) is a multisectoral approach among a dozen specialised agencies to address the daily living problems of a continent becoming poorer and more debt-shackled each day. Food, synchronised trading policies, high-tech and low-tech machinery and equipment, agricultural improvement projects, health and welfare aid are supplied together with building up a 'human resource bank' through education and training. More locally, drains are dug and river blindness epidemics stemmed in Burkina Faso, Zimbabwe's grain farmers are helped over bumper harvests and the need of better storage, and Zambia's school system is reorganised. The visions of 1945 have acquired operational focus.

The need of a 'globalised approach' is nowhere more true than in respect of the UN and the environment. It was mainly in the 1960s that the UN began to articulate and amplify a sense of anxiety about the careless exploitation of natural resources. We had a duty to conserve these resources and save the biosphere. A wide Earth-patriotism had to replace spasms of a narrower national sort. Many of the principles of concern that had reverberated from the Charter now acquired a deliberate 'green' tinge. Surveys and calculation became the tools of an Earthwatch. More graphically as forests were felled, seas were choked and deserts spread inexorably, brutal options became known as Doomwatch. World conferences in Stockholm in 1972 and in Rio de Janeiro in 1992 demonstrated once again a need to search for balance. Conference delegates from 178 governments and from NGOs echoed a call for a network of local, well-managed responses rather than for a sermon from 'the top down'. There were apparent in speech after speech at these conferences and in many UN publications, the beginnings of an attempt to redefine relationships between humans and nature and to do this in a specific, not an abstract, way.

The ideas and approaches and structures of the UN have been subjected to scrutiny over half a century. Sometimes the mirror reflects expectations clearly, at other times it is opaque. Many modifications of principle have been urged and implemented; the impossible is frequently called for. The width of engagement is tremendous fanning out from the first sentiments and suggestions of 1945. Fifty years show the UN succeeding, floundering, failing. Complexity, duplication, confusion, delay blunt the cutting edges. There are lessons for learning. There are questions for answering. There is time for trying. The chapters that follow will consider the blueprints and the pathways the UN has designed and blazed as it enters a new century.

3 Sovereign states as UN members

The contemporary UN is an institution 'on the up and up'. Measured in airtime or in press column inches its profile is now more visible and significant than it has ever been. There is more appreciation and informal discussion in the world outside. In general, disparagement is less common and much less strident. Gone are the divisions, acrimony and contemptuous cold-shouldering of former years. Among UN members there is more of a collective approach to problems and shared action. For almost forty years the Security Council was a ring for a heavyweight contest between the titans, the United States and the USSR, egged on by their partisan supporters. The General Assembly was a platform where rival faiths and policies were proclaimed or denounced. Silent and not-so-silent manoeuvres rigged the day's proceedings. As the year 2000 approaches a sea-change has overtaken the UN. Two of the formerly opposed superpowers have rediscovered the UN. There is now no need for the other 183 members to take refuge in contending lobbies. Is, though, the UN, as a 'thing in itself', able to carry aloft triumphantly and tirelessly the principles of the Charter? Or is the UN merely the sum of 185 parts? If it is the former, its conscience and willpower may ultimately transcend divisive state interests. If it is the latter, the disparate characteristics and interests of 185 members will be a potential for continued disunity. How does the UN deal with its sovereign state members? Which issues generate most controversy?

A good deal of the debate and controversy at the UN has centred on three main areas of activity, all to do with state sovereignty: the superpower contest, the problems of decolonisation, and the influential role of non-aligned states. Traces of all these may be detected still today. There are, of course, interconnections but to look briefly at the unravelling story helps us to see how united the contemporary UN has become.

THE SUPERPOWER CONTEST

Most conflict was aroused over ideological standpoints and because of incompatible interpretations of certain Charter principles such as sovereignty, domestic jurisdiction and the right of regional association. *Ideological standpoints* may be defined as elements of a belief system which a group professes and which is self-contained, consistent and self-justifying. Generally, this incorporates a world view and enables analysis, explanation and prediction of political and economic relationships in international society.

US expectations, ideologically backed, perhaps, now strike us as very optimistic, even evangelistic. The creation of a stable world order and the rehabilitation of a much shattered world would require US leadership. Experienced as a great war leader but not as a peace leader, the United States anticipated seeing the international collective expressing many of the open, democratic values proclaimed in the American Constitution. A world order conceived in a Charter would enunciate principles, define norms and do its best protectively to regulate a *status quo*. In this respect it could be said that a world assembly would be a forum for debating changes *within* the system rather than one changing the system itself. State sovereignty must be protected by requiring the consent of states as a prelude to action. If it came to collision over substantive issues risk could be lessened or precluded by some means of voting. The UN was to be an agent for moderate and constructive change: revolutionary, violent change was not wanted. As for economic matters, would not the best model be that of the global free market, whose virtues the United States had already proven? Specialised, technical agencies would address the needs of socio-economic betterment without political affiliation or interference. With all this in mind the United States was moving from the naïveté of isolationism to acting as the world's policeman and guarantor. Even in 1945, there was more than a trace of ethical prescription where the US-in-the-UN would support the Good and combat Darkness and Evil. (Many would argue that the inclination is still there today.)

Soviet expectations were a dramatic contrast. Delegates of the USSR brought with them heavy ideological baggage and displayed its contents frequently. The UN was to be solely a security organisation, a collective with a primary need to prevent renewed war. World order would be regulated mainly through treaties. The UN was to be an organisation subordinate to its member states. It would hardly be the voice of an independent conscience or common will. It would represent governments, not people, and governments were (and are) responsible for security. There would be a pragmatic need to maintain both a revolutionary outlook (the inevitability of struggle between Capitalism and the Proletariat) and the conservative one of preferring a *status quo*. Only that way might Progressives work with Imperialists. Economic and social change should be motivated by liberating people from discrimination and exploitation. International law was something about which one needed to be selective, particularly those aspects of it which legitimised Capitalist principles. All together, then and for many years, Soviet expectations of UN achievement were markedly lower than those of the United States.

It would always be difficult for such contrasted systems of belief to work together. Washington came to regard Moscow with ill-concealed distaste as a directive centre for expansion and intervention in democratic countries. In April 1950 Washington's National Security Council Planning Paper (NSC 68) was to brand the USSR as a 'slave society . . . animated by a new fanatic faith . . .'. This was to be resisted at all costs and by all means – at the UN and everywhere else. A march beyond Soviet boundaries, a 'creep of Communism', must be contained by words and, if necessary, even by force. Soviet speeches at the UN moved through resentment to forceful, often vitriolic denunciation of an anti-Soviet conspiracy led by the United States. Three decades of Cold War were to follow. US expectations were soured. Soviet pessimism was reinforced. In many quarters it was the UN, knee-deep in mire, that took the blame.

Sovereignty issues prised the superpowers apart. A theoretical definition of sovereignty is that it is the recognition by all states of a particular state's independence, territorial integrity and inviolability. Realistically, in legal eyes, it is the residuum of power which a state possesses within the confines laid down by international law. The UN in any case has to observe a distinction between fully independent sovereign states and those non-independent entities such as protectorates and dependent territories which lack sovereignty.

The sovereignty of the United States has always been fiercely protected. Fortress America reserved the right not to sacrifice any of its independence of judgement. Its position as a founder member of the UN must never be hostage to fortune when collective policies were contemplated. Even so, down the years, the United States came to recognise that membership of an international organisation imposes limitations on independent thought and enterprise. The Security Council, for instance, provided the protective device of the veto that could negate things the United States was not prepared to do: it could also prevent the United States doing what it did want to do.

And in the General Assembly the nation of forty-nine constituent statelets had only one voice and it became increasingly difficult to rally a majority. There was little doubt even then that the history of the UN would be, as Senator William Fullbright later put it, 'a history of retreat from false hopes and of adjustment to the reality of a divided world'. State-centred governments, provided they retained their autonomy, could get along together even though the universality of the Charter would not be easy to uphold. One way of subscribing to universality but remaining 'true to oneself' was to go for coexistence, a rational alternative to destructive confrontation. The UN, even if many of its initiatives were rendered immobile, was at least able to grow in numbers and to experiment with policies and programmes. Coexistence might be a way of managing international relations amid the permafrost of a Cold War but when the thaw occurred in 1979 the illusions of sovereign states were revealed. Madeleine Albright, America's UN Representative, told the Security Council in June 1973, 'The Cold War's end has removed the restraining, stabilising effect of the East–West nuclear standoff. Pent-up, often violent pressures for change have been released.' Was it not ironical, she inferred, that when there was less division between sovereign states, the UN, so states-centrist, was finding its membership becoming ever more chaotic?

Similarly, the instincts of the USSR were to put a closely guarded ring-fence around its policy making. Fortress Russia defended the home of 'Socialist solidarity' after the Second World War. Soviet insistence, when the Charter was being framed and for some years afterwards, was to stress the inviolability of states' frontiers and governmental autonomy. This position was rarely found convincing in the West in the light of clear evidence that Moscow placed great store on recruiting affiliates, either groups or individual 'fellow travellers', and that propaganda had to leap frontiers to do this. Indeed, during the 'McCarthy period' of the 1950s in the United States there were prominent accusations on Capitol Hill that US citizens in the service of the UN had been involved in subversive activity against their country, allegations that they were in the pay of Moscow. The UN might be a Trojan Horse and its personnel should be scrutinised. Each of the major powers accused the other of funding infiltration. In many a General Assembly debate in the 1950s and 1960s the explicit campaign of the USSR to embrace 'peace-loving peoples' was reckoned to have an aggressive purpose.

In brief, the struggle to affirm and to challenge sovereignty by both sides lacked consistency. There were many reasons behind these changes of front – the onrush of nuclear parity leading to moves for mutual understanding and *détente*, the questionable aspects of sovereignty demonstrated by the crises over Cuba or the Lebanon or Berlin or Hungary, speculative negotiations, either bilateral ones or hosted by the UN, where concessions were both sought and offered. A first firm stand was often to yield to expediency. In 1955 the Soviet leader, Nikita Khrushchev, had warned the Security Council that his country would 'never entrust the security of the Soviet Union to a foreigner'. This was to be the public image. Behind this screen there were many quite far-reaching explorations and understandings over arms control, West Germany, Berlin and Austria, each of which necessitated to some extent a lessening of irreducible sovereignty. In similar fashion President George Bush stated sternly in August 1988, 'A President can't subordinate his decision making to a multilateral body. He can't sacrifice one ounce of our sovereignty to any organisation.' Within two years the White House was urgently seeking UN decisions as to authorising moves against Iraq's invasion of Kuwait. Two years later, in December 1992, the US government was consulting the Security Council over possible intervention in Somalia by a US-led coalition to establish a secure environment for relief operations.

Some critics of the UN after superpower pretensions collapsed even declare statism to be anachronistic. They point to the intercontinental forces that breach the distinctiveness and security of all states. These are things such as satellite surveillance, global pollution, drug trafficking, strategic nuclear missiles, transnational corporations, financial marketing, AIDS, the flooding of refugees and economic migrants, the World Wide Web. Such problems do not need passports. A further curb on sovereign excess has been the vibrant growth of non-governmental organisations (NGOs).

Domestic jurisdiction is an important Charter principle and a key element of state sovereignty. Control by a state over people, land, resources, property within territorial limits was incontestable to the superpowers. After all, the notion of Keep Out was enjoined in Article 2.7 of the Charter which prohibited the UN interfering 'in matters essentially within the jurisdiction of a member state'. This warning seems deceptively simple. Is not each state the arbiter of what it regards as exclusive jurisdiction? Would the International Court of Justice have no say with its objective judgments and advice? How far are states likely to heed the comments and suggestions let alone the criticism of fellow members if these observations, as it were, cross frontiers? What matters are 'essential'? Essential to what?

The United States, ever since the time of the Monroe Doctrine of 1823, has nurtured the right to intervene in any part of the American Continent when 'vital interests' are considered endangered. Not surprisingly, and in the context of membership of an international body, these interests are notoriously difficult to define. In October 1962 the Kennedy Administration imposed a 'quarantine' or a selective blockade of Cuba to forestall reinforcement of Soviet-installed missile bases. Ostensibly, it was to prevent the furtherance of subversive activities. Washington's macho response over considerations of national security and prestige loomed larger than quieter and rather desperate negotiations between the UN Secretary-General and Premier Khrushchev. The superpowers eventually accepted settlement (partly including a trade-off of missile sites in Cuba against Turkey) while Castro's government in Cuba was stung and outraged at external interference in its affairs.

In the earlier years of the UN there were many occasions when the USSR asserted a right to intervene in countries where 'counter-revolutionary activity' either menaced the 'solidarity' of its satellites or posed an apparent threat to its own independence. From time to time the UN had to wrestle with complex factors which sparked crises over Czechoslovakia in 1948 and 1967, Hungary in 1956, Berlin in 1948–9 and 1958–61 – all occasions when the USSR appeared to advance westwards. There was continual tension over Soviet attitudes towards the independence of Poland and Yugoslavia. Outside the superpower relationship there was insistent condemnation of Israel, of dictatorship in Chile, and of apartheid in South Africa. The last instance of violated human rights and discussion of how best to bring pressure to bear even evinced some common feelings between the United States and the USSR; otherwise, there was much fear and confrontation in the Security Council and the General Assembly.

The contemporary UN rarely has to cope with states anguished because of political interference by others. The days of 'eloquent impotence' (as historian Michael Howard termed it) are largely over. Quite the reverse in many ways – the UN is being urged on all sides to 'go in' to save people from famine, violated basic human rights or to interpose between combatants in civil strife. Britain, France, Sweden and the former Soviet republics have sent contingents to many parts of the world as peacekeeping forces (as the next chapter describes). UN mandates have to be the result of invitation from states in trouble and there is punctilious respect for what must be understood as national sovereignty and jurisdiction. The names given to some of these operations such as *Operation Provide Comfort* in Northern Iraq in April 1991, *Operation Provide Promise* in Bosnia in 1993, *Operation Restore Hope* in Somalia after 1992 are all pointers to UN relief and resuscitation enterprise that goes over the parameters of sovereignty to rescue people *within*. There is a more forceful but equally penetrating mission in the use by the United States, Britain and France, acting under franchise to the UN, of 'no-fly zones' in southern Iraq and Bosnia.

Regional association as a principle hardly squares, one might think, with the ideal of collective security. As was pointed out in Chapter 1 the Charter did nothing to impair the inherent right of self-defence which is largely the aim of regional 'arrangements'. Going further than that, the Charter intimated that provided details of these schemes were known to the UN and that they were consistent with UN purposes and principles such arrangements might be used by the Security Council for enforcement action under its authority. Pacific action was, of course, the UN's way of working. It would take a good deal of space to discuss the ways in which this rather vaguely stated principle has been used by states and in particular how the superpowers, looking for footholds, firmed up the ground around themselves. The 1950s were a period of groups of states seeking a shield which often masked a sword. In 1949 NATO was formed. Contrariwise an Eastern shield (or umbrella) was put up by a group subscribing to the Warsaw Pact in 1955. The defence and consolidation needs of South East Asia were addressed by the South East Asia Treaty Organisation in 1954. Motivating forces here were 'encirclement' by the USSR and 'containment' by the United States and the West.

The UN was in no position to object to geopolitical strategies though the General Assembly frequently reverberated to speculation and heated debate about the military components of most regional associations. Two instances of force manipulating principle illustrate the dilemma in which the UN was placed when the intentions of the Charter were skewed. In October 1956 the USSR, solidly backed by its Eastern Bloc associates, sent an armed force into Hungary to overcome those who would overthrow the legitimate Communist government in Budapest. Savage fighting ensued. Condemnation of this in the Security Council was met by both the USSR and the UN's Hungarian delegate (rather surprisingly) refuting the condemnation and stating that an internal matter was no concern of the Western Powers or of the UN. One month later the scenario changed when the Hungarian government decided to ask the UN to put the dispute before the General Assembly where world opinion held sway and there was no veto. Almost predictably the Eastern Bloc came down with shrill denunciation and more troops. A new pro-Soviet government was installed. Nothing the UN could do by way of passing resolutions, through intensive negotiation, or through all the ingenious industry of Secretary-General Hammarskjöld, could shift the obduracy of the principle of regional association being misused. Moscow had apparently reckoned that political gains more than outweighed the costs in lost reputation and goodwill. Another example of dubious legality is that of the United States in April 1963 sending 10,000 Marines to the Dominican Republic to protect American lives and ensure that no Communist government could be established. Like the USSR and Hungary the United States justified intervention on the basis of an invitation from unofficial sources. Neither superpower wanted to see the UN at all closely involved in settling the crisis. The regional organisation in this case was the Organisation of American States (OAS). Invited by President Lyndon Johnson to help, the OAS actually split with five of its members most unhappy about the American landing. There was a furious discussion at the UN as to the advisability of a regional organisation being allowed to sideline an organisation charged in its Charter with responsibility for pacific conflict settlement. Although, as we have pointed out, such a regional organisation might be utilised by the UN, the OAS was in fact using military enforcement and politically heavy-handed tactics which were inflaming the situation and putting the UN in an impossible position. In the end the Secretary-General managed to smooth highly ruffled feelings. The United States did not block UN efforts at reconciliation as did the Russians over Hungary, and the UN managed to demonstrate that it was not prepared to see itself excluded by any regional organisation in circumstances where it had been appealed to.

THE PROBLEMS OF DECOLONISATION

Like peacekeeping this term is not in the UN Charter. The broad declaration in the Charter acknowledging the UN's responsibility to promote general advancement of dependent peoples is clear enough but the manner of its implementation has led to great controversy. One of the UN's proudest achievements has been to bring out of dependence more than eighty new sovereign states, many of them former colonies and trust territories.

Certainly, for the best part of twenty years after 1945 the UN witnessed powers like Britain, France, the Netherlands, Belgium and Portugal facing a growing barrage of protest and condemnation from representatives of small territories anxious to remove the shackles of Imperialist control. Their case was loudly taken up by the countries of Eastern Europe. The United States, moreover, was not at all happy to see a continuance of colonial rule. The urge for decolonisation was to charge those who clung to imperial pretensions with failing to make provision for social, political and economic development for many millions of people. It was a travesty of justice to affirm support for the Charter's faith in human rights while denying it in practice. A firm response from the rulers of empire was that constitutional advance was no matter for the UN but remained the prerogative of the administering power. Nor did they accept the UN's idea of setting targets for a grant of self-determination. All too easily supervision and inspection from New York would breach the principle of domestic jurisdiction. Basically, self-determination leading to self-government could be permitted when administering powers thought their dependent peoples were 'ready for it'.

Both administering powers and their critics recognised that decolonisation overnight presented dangers of undue haste – a disintegrating *status quo*, no infrastructure to facilitate economic advance, insufficient literacy and education to support political opportunity. Colonial powers sensed that their state of unpreparedness and unreadiness made it difficult to organise any credible move to disestablish power while their critics interpreted hesitation as sheer refusal to move at all. Colonialism must be eradicated was the cry. The 'Imperialists' claim that the UN should not even discuss paths towards self-determination was seen as a spurious device to cloak their unjust designs. The UN must go beyond soliciting promotion of human rights to intervention on behalf of exploited masses.

By 1960 the pace of decolonisation had quickened. Britain relinquished control of Ghana in 1957 and Nigeria followed in 1960. Seventeen former colonies, mainly in South East Asia, joined the UN in 1960. A Decolonisation Committee was established in New York in 1960 putting discussion of colonial affairs at the top of an agenda which dismissed the exclusivism of the administering powers. A Declaration on Decolonisation, also in 1960, proclaimed colonial rule to be incompatible with the Charter and international law. Were the universalistic principles of the UN to be set at naught by the selfish protective interests of certain powers? Discussion became heated. Independence movements in Indonesia and Malaysia and in Africa resorted to armed struggle in desperation. Violence in Rhodesia, Namibia, Angola and Mozambique flared into regional crises which were seen as threats to a wider peace.

The issue so often was not whether independence should be granted here or there but what was to be the rate of change? Colonial rulers found themselves not so much resisting pressure from member states in the General Assembly as having to retreat from a groundswell of informed and global public opinion. Could the French belief in a *mission civilisatrice* be credible if Paris continued to block debate over the Lebanon, Syria, Morocco, Algeria and Tunisia? When the French went on to boycott the General Assembly for a spell in 1955 the action aroused contempt in America and virulent criticism by African and Arab states. In Indonesia in 1945 the Netherlands refused to cede West New Guinea (West Irian) at first stating that the matter was purely a domestic one and that the outside world should not interfere. The General Assembly preference was for arbitration and for a UN Good Offices Committee to investigate Indonesian repudiation of 320 years of Dutch rule. A Security Council resolution in 1949 set up a commission with the task of building a constitution for a new federal community which would go through a process of transition to full authority. It was not until 1963 that a significantly named United Nations Temporary Executive Authority (UNTEA) aided by peacekeeping detachments was able to get an elected government into office and put through an assisted programme of social and economic development.

The midwife role of the UN in easing the birth of new communities in Indonesia and elsewhere in Cambodia and Namibia has raised many questions which continue to lack convincing answers. What do UN members understand by the term self-determination? Supposing that it is an absolute, inalienable right as the Charter presumes, then how is it to be exercised by a primitive, illiterate community? There have been problems with this in Indonesia, Angola, Ethiopia and Zaire, for instance, where the result of what might be thought to be premature enfranchisement has been a reversion to corruption and intimidation by a powerful junta. Elsewhere, for instance in Cyprus or in Israel, the successor to Britain's mandated territory, there has been scant obligation to confer equality of determination upon a minority. Decolonisation strategies have usually been to promote self-government by a state which acquires sovereignty. The former Secretary-General, Boutros Boutros-Ghali, believed the arrival of so many new states reconfirmed 'the importance and indispensability of the sovereign state as the fundamental entity of the international community' (*Agenda for Peace*, 1992). This sentiment is not easy to square with the tragic events of riven communities in Afghanistan, Cambodia, the Congo, Mozambique and Somalia.

More positively, perhaps, the great decolonisation movement has strengthened the UN and brought to it a wealth of cultures and imaginative resource. What might be thought of as follow-up activity occupies the specialised agencies of the UN night and day grappling with endemic poverty, the rights of women and of children, illiteracy, public health and economic revitalisation.

THE ROLE OF NON-ALIGNED STATES

Non-aligned states, many of them in the so-called Third World, have come to number more than half the UN roll. Their common interest has always been to steer clear of association with Great Power politics which they regard as polarising and destructive. They felt no need to pander either to the susceptibilities of the United States, sometimes bribed with dollars, or to Soviet rigidity of thinking, at times coupled with arm twisting. During the Cold War a common view in New York was that the 'non-aligneds' or 'uncommitteds' brought a breath of fresh air to the fetid sterility of General Assembly debate and, on occasion, to harsh Security Council encounters. Permanent members of the Security Council, on the other hand, were exasperated by their unconventional thinking, and dismayed by their 'unhelpful' neutrality.

The developing Third World has brought to the UN vibrant opinion stimulated by a common invective against exploitation but not always a consensus. These states have also forged alliances outside the UN, such as the Organisation of African Unity, the Islamic Conference, and the Association of South East Asian Nations (ASEAN), and they rely on careful, constant media representation and on occasional summits. Two groups make up the movement. First, there is the Non-aligned Movement itself, numbering 115 states, formed in Belgrade in 1961. Second, there is the so-called Group of 77, established after the United Nations Conference on Trade and Development (UNCTAD) held in Geneva in 1964. Now 120 states have joined their ranks. Both groups are intelligently directed and they can call upon a host of experts. Strategies employed combine ethics and cool-headed pragmatism. In the General Assembly and in UN committees and commissions support used to be given to goals and objectives of the 'committed' blocs on *particular* issues while refraining from siding diplomatically with any bloc on *all* issues. Temporary diplomatic and economic coalitions have given these movements resilience and encouragement. The Group of 77 works powerfully at UN trade conferences to increase its influence on industrial nations. For the non-aligned, minimising dependence upon larger states may help bolster confidence at home in national unity and in the sensible discrimination shown by their leaders.

Scandinavia has sent generations of independently minded delegates to the UN, while India, Egypt, Fiji, Costa Rica, Malta, Tanzania and Senegal on many occasions have taken a lead in seeking to breach the log jams of UN controversy. They have been active and constructive in their attitudes to the Korean War in 1950–3, the Congo dispute in 1960, the Suez adventure of Britain, France and Israel in 1956, US interventions in Central America, Israel's harsh treatment of its Arab neighbours, the excesses of apartheid in South Africa, the treatment of Jews in the Soviet Union, Britain's war with Argentina over the Falklands in 1982, the Iraq–Iran battles of 1980–4, the Soviet invasion of Afghanistan in 1979. Their concern to make the world free of nuclear weaponry has been resolute and influential.

Quite significantly, the non-aligned states have transferred majorities in the General Assembly from the United States and the West to the developing world (sometimes with heavy backing from Eastern Europe's Socialist states). Pride of place must be given to socio-economic concerns. As early as 1960 the delegate for Pakistan told the General Assembly, 'A revolution of rising expectations is sweeping through these countries. Fatalism and resignation have given way to expectation and demand.' No wonder then that the developing states in 1974 put up a stern challenge to Capitalist fixity with their demand for a New International Economic Order. Partnership would replace patronage. Regulation by the well-off states must give way to new ways of bringing the poor into managerial roles through improved trade terms, reduction of debt, and transfer of skills and technology. Otherwise, the poor would be revolutionaries rather than customers. The suggested reform did not appeal to the protective instincts of well-endowed states. And in this connection it has to be noted that some non-aligned members such as OPEC and one or two Pacific Rim states are particularly protective and keen on their sovereignty. The point, however, was well made even if the main economic cleavage these days is between an affluent North and a disadvantaged South.

THE UN AND THE FUTURE OF STATISM

As the 1990s draw to a close the question comes up again: how is the UN in an interdependent world to deal with the distinctiveness of 185 member states? What is the future of statism? A number of issues arise. First, what will replace the old superpower rivalry of the Cold War? The contemporary easement of ideology at the UN, with its real chance of stability and trust, mostly dates from Mikhail Gorbachev's address to the UN General Assembly in December 1988. 'The primacy of universal human values', he declared, 'has been substituted for the battle between Communism and democratic capitalism.' Will, though, this replacement endure? Some polarised tensions remain in what many claim is now a unipolar society, for example US wariness over a majority in the General Assembly which may not go its way, disenchantment over UN internal management and finance, and doubts about intervention and domestic jurisdiction. The potential expansion of NATO eastwards might also revive old rivalries and tensions among countries in Eastern Europe formerly associated with the USSR.

Second, decolonisation procedures, in some pessimistic views, have opened up a can of worms. Fragmented, disputed sovereignty questions appear on every General Assembly agenda. The question is urgent: in what ways can young states work with others without compromising their own legitimate independence? Enfranchisement confers autonomy but a state, economically undeveloped and buffeted by harsh, external market forces, may well find sovereignty a delusion offering little in the way of independence or added resource. Third, and a philosophical point, how far can there be an assurance that a UN member state represents a collective good for its citizens? This sentiment is clearly enunciated in the UN Charter. Yet, in places like Angola, Burma, Nigeria, Rwanda and parts of Latin America many people, perhaps millions of them, have come to regard their state as an oppressive manager of elitist power and privilege. That is far from the spirit of the UN Charter. It is not easy to see how this problem may be resolved. From time to time there have been suggestions that any state seeking admission to the UN should, before acceptance, prove to the Organisation both its impartiality (nonalignment) and the extent of its domestic observance of justice and human rights.

Finally, sovereign states are here to stay. More tolerance will be needed. The UN Secretary-General in his *Agenda for Peace* in 1992 put the matter in these terms:

> The time of absolute and exclusive sovereignty, however, has passed: its theory was never matched by reality. It is the task of leaders of states today to understand this and to find a balance between the needs of good governance and the requirements of an ever more interdependent world.

Within this context it can be claimed that the UN has adapted to changing realities in numerous ways in the first fifty years of its existence. This, indeed, has been the focus of Part I of this book. Priorities for the future, however, will be different and it is these priorities that will be the concern of Part II and Part III of the book.

Part II

The UN in a changing international environment

4 Peacekeeping

How does today's world regard the UN as a peacekeeper? What distinctive principles underlie the task? What methods are commonly employed? With changes in the international environment such as the relaxed grip of the Cold War confrontation, the doubling of world population, the flooding of lethal weaponry everywhere, the migrations of 23 million refugees, the rise of nationalism and fundamentalism, with changes of this nature and magnitude should things be done differently? Contemporary opinion, as the media mirrors it, seems to regard peacekeeping in three lights: horror, confusion and criticism.

The harrowing of Balkan villagers, Iraq's Highway to Hell, the famine in Somalia are all seen with part horror and part incredulity. Public response is frequently confused, ranging from a call for action to restore security and sanity, to a fatalistic echo that nothing can be done. Understandably, peacekeeping gets a bad press. Criticism frequently points to somebody else doing too much or too little. Peacekeeping missions seem to be evaluated only in terms of their immediate achievements. Peace is a long-term process. If peacekeeping is defined as assisting disputing parties to reach agreement and then implement accord, and if this must be done without using force, then many criticisms voiced appear ill-informed and impatient. Enforcement of peace must be the last resort of the peacekeeper. It scarcely helps to urge the peacekeeper to adopt a 'bomb and talk' approach as was obvious over the Gulf War and Bosnia.

PEACEKEEPING'S CHANGING AGENDA

As the world approaches the end of the second millennium the UN is clearly modifying its agenda in regard to maintaining peace in five main ways:

1 The UN Charter saw peace (collective security) being kept by five permanent members (the 'Great Defenders') cooperating with all other members. This belief was steadily cut away by the Cold War. The concept of the 'neighbourhood watch', identifying actual or potential aggressors and then dealing with dispute and conflict, was superseded by nervous postures to prevent the 'trigger-happy' Great Powers from shooting first. Peacekeeping has frequently assumed the form of collective defence rather than collective security.
2 The notion of global peace has fragmented into rather desperate concern to stem or deflate crises bubbling up in sensitive regions, for instance Europe, the Middle East, South East Asia. Peacekeeping has been concerned often with damage limitation or mopping up after violence.
3 The UN Charter of 1945 set out procedures in its Chapter VI for settling disputes peacefully *before* conflict and in Chapter VII action to restore peace *after* conflict. Time and again preventive and restorative action moves into peacekeeping operations out in the field, away from the New York forum. Each operation has needed differing guidelines and management. Peacekeeping over the years has become more dynamic, pragmatic and controversial.
4 Peacekeeping *between* nations (the spirit of the UN Charter) has increasingly become peacekeeping *within* nations. Yet, eighty-nine out of ninety-two conflicts during 1990–5 have been due to internal feuding. Charter articles specifically forbid the UN to intervene 'in matters which are essentially within the domestic jurisdiction of any state'. They acknowledge the inherent right of individual or collective self-defence. They do not rule out the use of appropriate regional 'arrangements'. As a consequence, as we shall see later, effective, swift and impartial peacekeeping has often run into difficulty.
5 The founders' ideal of the UN having 'teeth', a standby force to carry out peacekeeping, has never materialised. As we have noted above there is frequently a sense of frustration and futility at the scale of conflicts and violations and impatience to secure results. After many years of recruiting for operations on an *ad hoc* basis there is now more discussion of the possibilities of training and maintaining UN troubleshooting groups, highly mobile ones, able to deploy carefully and effectively.

BASIC TYPES OF PEACEKEEPING

Fifty years of UN activity have taken three main forms: preventive diplomacy, preventive deployment, and peacebuilding.

Preventive diplomacy strategies rely on diplomatic and negotiating methods to deal with disputes and threats and prevent them from developing into armed conflict. Generally, this is an approach *before* conflict.

Preventive deployment strategies, on the other hand, aim at deterring parties from escalating a dispute into armed conflict. This is a military response involving soldiers taking up positions between opponents and using observing, monitoring and reporting techniques. Additionally, such personnel will assist in furnishing law and order, providing relief and protection, maintaining essential services. In most respects, this is a securing operation *after* conflict or when it is thought to be imminent.

Peacebuilding – the widest and longest perspective – takes the form (a) globally, of designing, codifying and implementing international laws and agreements, and (b) locally, of reconstructing political, economic and social structures usually after violation and destruction. Techniques may include peace broking and ambitious and cooperative programmes of rehabilitation.

THE RATIONALE OF PEACEKEEPING

If peacekeeping is not referred to by name in the UN Charter, it is implicit in most of its chapters. One could say that it has developed out of the Charter as an approach to underpin the main purpose of the UN, namely the maintenance of international peace and security through preventing conflict, controlling an outbreak of hostilities and promoting peaceful settlement. The Security Council has the main responsibility for this. It has the task of identifying any threat to peace, a breach of it, or any act of aggression and then to call upon parties to settle a dispute peacefully. In Chapter VII of the UN Charter a whole range of possibilities is listed – negotiation, enquiry, mediation, conciliation, arbitration, judicial settlement. The help of some regional body may be needed. If things get nowhere Chapter VII provides for collective action in the field. To give authority to this there must be endorsement from nine out of the Council's fifteen members, including all of the five permanent members. The UN Secretary-General (more Secretary than General) has to confer as to the makeup of any force, its cost, and the nature of its deployment.

Peacekeepers may be sent out as unarmed observers, assigned to scrutinise a situation and report back on it to New York. They may be instructed to monitor a troop withdrawal, supervise a cease-fire, patrol buffer zones, see to the disarming of combatants. They may have to ensure the implementation of an agreement or the organisation of a plebiscite or an election. Should conflict spark into violence the peacekeeper escorts food and medical supplies to threatened civilians, and is indispensable in regard to first aid, refugee reception, the maintenance and repair of transport and other essential facilities. Peacekeepers despatched on missions abroad will wear the uniform of their own state and a beret or steel helmet, blue in colour with the insignia 'UN'. They are the 'Blue Berets'. As catalysts for peace, not instruments of war, they are responsible to UN oversight but remain under national command in matters to do with discipline, equipment and pay. Their job is not that of normal soldiering. Persuasive ability, patience and tact take precedence over combat skills and these have been amply demonstrated since 1948 by 71,000 men and women forming the backbone of thirty-six peacekeeping and observer missions. Associated peacekeeping work by civilians, technical specialists, policemen and women, election scrutineers has involved an estimated 650,000 people from seventy countries. More than 1,000 of them have lost their lives.

Certain conditions are held to be essential for successful peacekeeping:

- Intervention is only possible with the cooperation and consent of the 'host' state.
- Clear objectives should be detailed in a comprehensive mandate and translated into adequate resources, that is personnel, equipment and funds. There must be a sustained will to provide these means and to keep on doing so.
- Impartiality on the part of a multinational body – not easy in complex, active roles. Force is not to be used except in self-defence. Never must it be a win-or-lose situation.
- Management and operational strategies should be closely coordinated. Fast interlocking factors in a situation need effective intelligence gathering, flexible procurement and careful logistics.
- Continued understanding and back-up – guarantees from a majority of UN members and on the ground careful liaison with local people. Peacekeepers must be allowed free movement and access to facilities.
- Long-term peacekeeping and peace-making should specify the shape of a programme from cease-fire to agreed means of rehabilitation.

- A 'sunset clause' defines outcome, criteria for termination (an 'exit plan'), contingency schemes for scale-down, even withdrawal and evacuation.

Mandates assigned to peacekeeping forces are complex and variable with the prime impulses those of prevention and relief. (See the 'Guide to further reading' for reference to fuller listing and discussion and the list of acronyms referring to peacekeeping operations.) Enforcement missions are discussed later in this chapter. These are some of the thirty-six peacekeeping operations launched since 1948:

Observation, monitoring, truce supervision:
Middle East (1948–), Lebanon (1958), Dominican Republic (1965–6), Israel–Syria (1974), Iran–Iraq (1988–91), Afghanistan (1988–90), Angola (1988–91), Central America (1989–), Iraq–Kuwait (1991–), Western Sahara (1991–), Mozambique (1992–), Uganda–Rwanda (1993–).

Interposition:
India–Pakistan frontier (1949–), Egypt–Sinai (1956) (1973–9), Congo (1960–4), Yemen (1963–4), Cyprus (1964–), Lebanon (1978–), former Yugoslavia (1992–), Somalia (1992–3), Macedonia (1995–).

Election supervision, national rebuilding:
West Irian (1962–3), Namibia (1989–90), Western Samoa (1991), Cambodia (1991–2), former Yugoslavia (1996).

THE ENFORCEMENT OF PEACE

Enforcement operations such as Korea 1950–3 and the Gulf War 1991 were not peacekeeping as we have defined earlier. Multinational coalition forces, appropriately equipped, were despatched to Korea and the Gulf with a stern mandate to deal with aggression by one state against another. Chapter VII of the UN Charter in Article 42 does provide for the use of force if pacific measures have proved unavailing. If it is judged that a state's internal security has imploded and that this represents a threat to wider security then missions are sent as they were in 1993 to Rwanda and to Somalia. Enforcement from UN headquarters may be exercised by a system of sanctions levelled to induce settlement or force compliance with objectives already decided by the UN. Complete or partial embargoes on goods, transport and services materially affected South Africa particularly in 1977 and 1984. This may well have helped to bring an end to the noxious creed of apartheid. Iraq was heavily penalised in this way in 1990 and Yugoslavia denied arms from abroad. In 1992 sanctions were imposed on Somalia, Libya and Cambodia. Yet, sanctions raise questions. Are sanctions levied against a whole population fair? Do they not provide a focus for resentment and stiffened resolve when harm to vulnerable civilians is clear? Moreover, 'sanctions busting' is a very profitable and dishonourable trade. How far can it be controlled?

ENFORCEMENT: KOREA AND THE GULF

A brief account of some of these operations gives food for thought. If they were not actually peacekeeping proper, why have the actions in Korea (1950–3), the Gulf (1991), Somalia (1991–5) and Bosnia (1992–) been so unhelpful in their conception, execution and consequences? The first two have certain characteristics in common. They were both actions by coalitions which the UN, as it were, put out to franchise. They were both led and directed by the United States. Each response was triggered by condemnation of apparently simple aggression. In rather different ways the Korean and Gulf operations were strategic thrusts to restore a *status quo* which was held to guarantee stability within a region. In the case of Korea, an anti-Communist salient had to be rescued from attack. In the Gulf crisis, a vital part of the world's oil supplies appeared imperilled. An element of power-gaming in both instances seems to have little to do with the implementation of UN Charter principles. Certain aspects of these operations raise controversial and uncomfortable issues. Enforcement fire-power was very considerable. In Korea the Americans led a coalition of sixteen states providing half the troops, 86 per cent of the naval force and 90 per cent of the air force. Fifty years later against Iraq a coalition of twenty-one states fielded 680,000 troops of whom two-thirds were from the United States. This time it was incomparably high-tech, short, swift and very brutal and it cost $70,000 million. The immediate objective of stopping the fighting and blocking further aggression was achieved. Peace was enforced but in its fullest sense, that is to help people feel secure and representatively governed, peace was never effected. In Korea three years of battle and eight years of fitful negotiation brought nothing other than a nation divided north and south under rival patronage. The Gulf saw the conflict blasted into cease-fire and armistice but with no end to Saddam Hussein's dictatorial arrogance and the destabilising behaviour of Iraq. The questions remain. Why was the UN sidelined with so little exploration of a range of settlement possibilities? Was there no prospect of a sanctions system being applied? The exigencies of the Cold War forced the pace over Korea and made it unlikely that the United States, determined to 'contain' Communist expansion, would wait lamely for cumbersome UN procedures requiring objectivity, law and restraint. In the case of the Gulf there was an urge to pre-empt any turbulent threat to assured oil supplies. Does peacekeeping in these instances become a prisoner of political expediency?

ENFORCEMENT: SOMALIA

A mission to aid Somalia in the spring of 1991 soon went badly wrong. At the outset, humanitarian considerations prompted an international relief effort to stall the terrible consequences of famine in a state where all authority had collapsed. For over twelve months, a UN peacekeeping force, UNOSOM, struggled with a mandate to restore order, to monitor an arms embargo against feuding warlords and also attempt to disarm combatants. An element of compulsion was thought advisable and to provide this the Security Council authorised the landing of a US-led force, UNITAF, whose 38,000 troops would 'beef up' the security task. Food supplies were soon safe but almost predictably the heavy presence of so many 'foreigners' with evident battle strength inflamed Somali opinion. This UN operation, termed 'Operation Restore Hope', raised political temperatures and violence ensued. When the armed UNITAF was replaced in 1993 by 15,000 UNOSOM II personnel it was hoped that their less visible element of force would present a more peaceful UN undertaking. Unfortunately, the killing of twenty-three Pakistani soldiers in one incident in June brought a punitive kickback from the peacekeepers whose US soldiers were accused of using excessive force. The operation was now doomed to fail. Through the autumn of 1993 and into 1994 the peacekeepers were hemmed into a compound from which they could hardly emerge. There was no prospect of any stable Somali government. The Security Council with unusual candour declared that the Somalian operation was not functioning as a peacekeeping enterprise should. Contending parties were not disarmed and there was no chance of reconciliation between them, at least with outside help. Neither the UN nor any regional body like OAU or OPEC was able to bring pacifying influence to bear. By March 1995 UNOSOM II had to leave. The attempt at enforcement in Somalia raises a number of demanding issues. What were the long-term objectives as distinct from immediate holding of the ring? Were the rules of engagement in this pacification and relief exercise too imprecise, perhaps too forceful eventually? Is there a point at which frustration and retaliatory instincts lead to peacekeepers crossing the threshold of violence? Should a termination date have been fixed using criteria of success and failure (if it is possible to establish these)?

ENFORCEMENT: FORMER YUGOSLAVIA

A third instance of peacekeeping by enforcement is that of Bosnia-Herzegovina–Croatia in 1992–7. The anguish of this experience has taught the world a great deal about the possibilities and limitations of peacekeeping, UN style. The first impulse of UN member states was to send in an international force of 26,500 Blue Berets (UNPROFOR) in February 1992 with a mandate to monitor a ceasefire in Croatia, to supervise Yugoslav army withdrawal and to protect civilian and UN personnel in Bosnia. Sanctions were levied by the Security Council against aggressor Serbs and an arms embargo imposed. Negotiations by UN mediators and others did not prevent stage-by-stage takeover of territory and the forced eviction of those regarded as 'ethnically impure'. Eight cease-fires failed to hold. Targeting of civilians rendered the objective of protection an empty concept. Areas designated 'safe' and ringed with exclusion zones for demilitarisation were systematically violated. In any case, UNPROFOR's resources had been niggardly provided by many UN members. Inevitably, peacekeeping by persuasion moved into an enforcement mode using NATO air strikes. Predictably, this tore away the impartiality posture of the UN, and it enraged, particularly, the Serbs.

In late 1995 the Clinton Administration decided to intervene to resolve the festering Bosnian crisis. The three Presidents of the warring factions were airlifted to the United States. There they were confined for two weeks at the Air Force base at Dayton, Ohio, and subjected to continuous question and answer. This novel form of peace seeking yielded fruit – the Dayton Agreement. With a cease-fire overall, a NATO force of 60,000, to be known as I-FOR, would take over from UNPROFOR on 19 December 1995. Heavily armed policing and stern engagement rules would underpin a constitutional reform establishing a unitary state of Bosnian–Serb partnership and eventually elections. Social and economic rehabilitation and the resettlement of refugees was to follow.

But employment of bigger sticks and carrots has brought about a fragile stand-off on the ground since the beginning of 1996. The question remains: a peacekeeping force with only a temporary deployment can keep people apart but will it be able to force them to live harmoniously? The Dayton Agreement was envisaged as giving the UN an opportunity to deploy its UN Development Programme using the experience and skills of its specialised agencies and the investment schemes of the World Bank. Alternatively, an accord which the US press saw as 'signed, sealed and undelivered' might founder because the mix of military and civilian effort is not quite right and costs have been underestimated. Already, the international operation has cost more than $4 billion excluding the costs of civilian reconstruction. Half of the military bill is being met by the United States; Britain's share is $4 million. None of this can be recovered because the Bosnian operation has passed out of exclusive UN sponsorship. Nor is the account closed. From December 1996 the peacekeeping mission statement loses its enforcement tone and reads as *stabilisation* (succeeding *implementation* and *protection*). The new peacekeeping force, S-FOR, is scaled down to 30,000 troops. It will all be an expensive and time-intensive exercise, an attempt at peacebuilding which will require a sustained and multifaceted rehabilitation programme to inch the people of former Yugoslavia towards tolerance and collaboration.

PEACEKEEPING AS ANAESTHETIC: CYPRUS

In the instances described above momentum acquired a destructive character. Cyprus, on the other hand, has been *tranquillised* for thirty-one years. The original 1964 mandate, a maintenance schedule, authorised UNFICYP's 6,000 peacekeepers to use patrols and observation posts, 140 of them, to keep an eye on flash-points between rival Greek Cypriots and Turkish Cypriots and to work for restored normality. Eight out of ten Cypriots are strongly partial to a 1,500 year link with Greece, two out of ten prefer allegiance to mainland Turkey and some form of self-determination for their own community. Peacekeeping has been possible only through partitioning the island of Cyprus. Can peace ever be built within a divided state? Korea demonstrates that this is unlikely with parties to a contest armed materially and ideologically by outside patrons. Here in Cyprus, Greece and Turkey, both NATO members, look on ominously still. In July 1974 the UN's ten years of patrolling a 'Green Line' were thrown into precipitate danger when Turkey exchanged its fretful stand-off for invasion of Cyprus and occupation of the northern third of the island. The UN force could only look on at the rapid dispersal of refugees from the disputed zones as more than 200,000 Greek Cypriots fled south and 40,000 Turkish Cypriots moved in to their own proclaimed republic. A Greek majority viewed the UN operation as helping them restore authority over a disloyal Turkish element. Turkish Cypriots believed the peacekeepers to be shoring up an oppressive regime. The UN personnel in the middle maintained peace in a high degree of alertness which coped with violence and impeded access only through exercising a remarkable degree of patience, foresight, initiative and forbearance. Trust and goodwill among all Cypriots had to be laboriously built. UNFICYP, however, was a fire brigade or a first-aid post, managing *ad hoc* short-term relief, not the treatment of underlying causes of conflict.

From time to time there is the suggestion that setting a final date on UNFICYP presence and programming its withdrawal will bring quarrelsome Cypriots to a conclusive solution. There seems little evidence for that. An indefinite *status quo* becomes more acceptable to both sides than compromises needed for final resolution.

PEACEKEEPING REAPPRAISED

To declare that we are all peacekeepers now is not just to utter a naïve truism. How best can states as members of the UN meet the challenges of the changing international environment? Much thought is being given to this, particularly since the UN Secretary-General Boutros Boutros-Ghali put out a number of suggestions for reform in his *Agenda for Peace* in 1982.

Preventive diplomacy should be given top priority. An early-warning system would use high-tech information gathering and analysis. Preventive diplomacy teams networking the information could subject it to expert appraisal, communicate between a central conflict centre and regional units, recruit mediatory skills (especially third-party help), and decide appropriate action – diplomatic, legal, investigatory, possibly military participation. Decisions as to enforcement would be critical.

Security Council consideration and authorisation would be wider and more representative of UN members' views if the Council were expanded and if the permanent members' monopoly were 'diluted'. Multitrack diplomacy would certainly benefit from improved liaison with regional bodies, NGOs, research institutions, technical expertise. There is room for experiment and innovation here.

Clearer criteria for intervention are needed, for example do observation and report reveal everyday life to be under direct, widespread threat? Further, is there any prospect of alleviation by responsible internal authorities? Preventive deployment needs careful and frequent policy formulation. Mandates should outline aims cogently and provide for modification and even termination. A deterrent function must be very clearly described as to desirable scale, resources and time. Associated tasks such as monitoring, observation, protection, relief, demobilisation and so on are to be detailed. The need to work with changing terms of reference in the event of crisis must be acknowledged. Particularly important here would be the availability of specially trained vanguard units held by member states on a stand-by basis – an idea that has been around for fifty years.

Peacekeeping will be sterile and short-lived without peacebuilding. Initial responses by the UN have been termed 'timely, graduated and effective' if they are seen to make progress with conflict resolution. If, though, a state of peace is held to be those circumstances which satisfy basic human needs (safety, shelter, food, employment, etc.) then the restoration and revitalisation of a community is likely to require very great resources, imagination and effort. Peacebuilding will need elaborate coordination of programmes initiated and sustained by UN specialised agencies, NGOs, and other means of relief and development. The resourcing of peacekeeping needs scrutiny and improvement. Peacekeeping's annual budget is some $3.7 million. A single enforcement operation like that of the Gulf War coalition may cost twenty times that. (It has been estimated that the annual cost of UN peacekeeping is roughly the same as the cost of one and a half days of the 1991 Operation Desert Storm in Iraq.) Costs are rising but they are still a great deal less than what is spent on arms procurement by the developed and developing world. (Some 80 per cent of the weaponry is supplied by the Security Council's five permanent members. The Guardians of Peace as envisaged in the UN Charter have become the furnishers of war.) Alternative sources of revenue for peacekeeping can be explored. There might be a levy on arms sales, borrowing from the IMF or from the World Bank. A levy on international air transport is one suggestion. Undoubtedly there is scope for reviewing ways in which funds are assigned to certain projects. More careful cost-and-benefit auditing and more decentralisation are possible.

The contemporary world is dramatically one of violence and gross human disparities. Nevertheless, the chances of former adversaries and political partisans working together as peacekeepers and peace-builders have never been greater since the early 1990s swept away so much of the enmity of the Cold War epoch. The need now is for nations united in purpose to translate intentions and priorities into action. Keeping the peace depends upon keeping out of war. Nations must come together to control their weaponry. This is the topic of the next chapter.

5 Arms control and disarmament

Many might say that the UN has been no more successful with controlling arms than with keeping the peace. Fifty years have seen little progress but tortuous discussion, evasion and double-talk, especially by the permanent members of the Security Council. Meanwhile, at a global level, states on average spend $1 million a minute on war weapons. At that rate control of some sort becomes a priority if a civilised world is to survive.

It is important to distinguish disarmament from arms control. The former is the process of renouncing or generally eliminating weapons systems; control measures, on the other hand, seek to limit or restrain the production, testing, deployment and use of particular weaponry together with measures which build confidence and security between states. Disarmament is a radical proposition. Not surprisingly, the contemporary world shows little tangible understanding of disarmament as a total process, though with control there is encouraging movement as the result of bilateral action by superpowers, or by regional groups of smaller powers, or by the UN as sponsor and observer.

Factors bearing upon arms control have been altered significantly by several interrelated changes in international politics. The decline of the Cold War after forty years of adversarial posturing has led powers to cool if not melt down aspects of their armouries. Correspondingly, there has been convergence by former rivals on possibilities of control, frequently with the UN in the chair. Nevertheless, the world has seen increased reliance on small arms and their delivery systems by smaller client states. Overall, the priorities of arms limitation have switched from the need of macrocontrol (e.g. of nuclear weapons) to microcontrol (e.g. conventional weapons, smaller in scale and wider in scope). This chapter will look briefly at the UN agenda and then at progress made in a number of weapons areas. Finally, the question is posed: are fifty years of experience and experiment showing signs of success?

THE UN AGENDA

In accordance with the basic UN Charter principle to maintain peace and security without resort to force (Article 11) the General Assembly recommends measures to govern the regulation of armaments. The Security Council, responsible for peace and security, 'with the least diversion for armaments of the world's human and economic resources', has to formulate plans for regulation (Article 26) and 'to implement such action as may be necessary to maintain or restore international peace and security' (Articles 42–9). A Military Staff Committee was to be the instrument for the UN in this action mode. Political impasse, unfortunately, has not set this process in gear.

The UN, in a first flush of optimism in the 1950s, set up an Atomic Energy Commission in 1946 and a Commission for Conventional Arms in 1947. On account of the deepening Cold War, progress became soured and stultified. The following years saw the reign of the Balance of Terror with the nuclear monopoly of the major powers (the 'Magic Circle'). Mutually assured destruction (MAD) became a defence matrix within which control possibilities remained inert. The main thrust of UN activity has been to focus attention on specific problems, to sponsor resolutions and to initiate discussion and study. Disarmament Decades and Special Sessions have amplified anxieties and the forceful opposition of much scientific and public opinion. The forty-member UN Conference on Disarmament meeting in Geneva each year for six months can only advise and promote, not dictate to, sovereign states each eyeing vulnerability and competitive advantage. In particular, for half a century the world has tried to come to grips with twin challenges: nuclear proliferation and nuclear testing.

NUCLEAR PROLIFERATION

At least fifty countries, nearly one in four UN members, employ nuclear energy. Twenty of these are termed Nuclear Weapon States (NWS) if they exploded a nuclear device before 1 January 1967. These are the five permanent members and others such as India, Pakistan, North and South Korea, South Africa, Brazil, Egypt and Iraq. Non-nuclear Weapon States (NNWS) are regarded as states with a potential who may be tempted to cross the threshold. Clouding these awesome realities are the fears that others may be drawn into the ring as well as the hazards of military diversion, of radiation seepage and pollution, of sabotage, and inefficient management and processing.

The UN set up the International Atomic Energy Authority (IAEA) in Vienna in 1957. Two tasks were given. The first was to accelerate and enlarge the contribution of nuclear energy to global peace, prosperity and health. The second was the institution of a safeguards system to ensure that energy sources would not be used for military ends. Codes of practice and rigorous standards were to address the first need, otherwise the system of safeguards was locked into audit, report and inspection. Vienna was to keep meticulous records of all aspects of nuclear science and technology. One hundred states agreed to be bound in this way.

In the 1950s and 1960s the UN General Assembly was 'running after the bus' as the superpowers built up competing nuclear stocks. Somehow control had to be not just a block on nuclear transfer from haves to have-nots, rather, it should be an essential element in a broader scheme for disarmament. This point was not easily taken by Moscow, suspecting that the United States would never 'build down' its monopoly. Nor were sovereign states willing to submit to intrusive investigation and limitation schemes. As for NNWS there was an apprehension that forgoing a nuclear potential would add to their 'vulnerability and disadvantage them economically. Moreover, without firm security guarantees by way of compensation they would lose the benefit of armed alliance with others.

From time to time there were auspicious gains in bringing about a degree of security either in particular geographical zones or in restrictions on the deployment of specific weapons systems. The UN was successful in getting an Antarctic Treaty in 1959 which declared Antarctica to be a Nuclear Weapons Free Zone (NWFZ). In 1964 twenty-three Latin American nations signed the Tlatelolco Treaty, as a further edict against military nuclear proliferation. Outer space was designated a zone for peaceful use only in 1967 by 113 states. The Indian Ocean was declared a Zone of Peace in 1971. And 1972 brought two important treaties, one for the sea bed beyond the twelve-mile zones of territorial waters and a Biological Weapons Convention attempting to crack down on alternative weaponry.

More than ten years of earnest discussion, bargaining and tabling of draft schemes in the New York UN headquarters and in Vienna finally produced a Non-proliferation Treaty (NPT) in 1968. Now there existed legislation for the original objectives of the IAEA, namely that of peaceful promotion of nuclear energy and the supervised prevention of illicit use of nuclear technology. However, the only possible route for agreement was to affirm publicly that all states had an inalienable right of access to nuclear 'know-how' provided they proved their willingness and readiness to work for the cessation of the arms race. Every five years there would be a review conference. States signing the Treaty now number 175, while 195 NGOs and research institutions have a form of affiliation.

Throughout almost thirty years of the NPT review process a number of reservations and questions surface constantly. There is much resentment about the reluctance of the major powers to relinquish 'that old black magic' of nuclear dominance. Many regard such peace promotion as belonging to the realm of fantasy. In this light, the NPT may be regarded as a staged, agreed limitation of what there *is* among the NWS rather than mandatory elimination of what there *might be* among the NNWS. The latter feel hostage to misfortune when the NWS ignore the Treaty's Chapter V which requires all participants actively to promote disarmament. Then there are the safeguards. How far are they able to prevent covert nuclear activities and, in the worst case, take decisive action against offenders? UN monitoring is in place but perhaps it needs a more sophisticated web of satellites, and other instruments of detection. In addition to the dumping of radioactive waste and the transhipment of toxic materials, which are not always easy to detect, there is a search for alternative means of production to acquire or regain nuclear capability, all this in the guise of modernisation. Other forms of proliferation are illicit trading in fissile materials, clandestine enrichment to weapons-grade of reactor-grade uranium, and a brain drain of personnel from former Warsaw Pact partner states. Again, peaceful conversion of production facilities is likely to be uncertain and sporadic.

Political factors, too, bear upon the implementation of the NPT. With the retreat of the Cold War, nuclear dominance is less easy to depend upon given the risk that even small adversaries in a regional conflict (e.g. the Gulf in 1991) might use nuclear arms. The security of major powers once depended on war winning; now it is war avoidance. Political fault lines have fragmented. Russia now has four constituent republics sharing half of the old Soviet stockpile of 27,000 warheads.

In 1995 the NPT was put to its signatories for possible unconditional and indefinite extension. China, wanting 'a smooth extension', even undertook as a sign of grace to abandon the option of first use of a nuclear weapon. Stern questions remained. In what circumstances do states consider themselves so irreversibly threatened that they can justify the use of a nuclear weapon as a means of defence? At the final review conference in 1995 it was very strongly stated that unless all the major powers and all the other NWS renounced the possibility of pre-emptive strikes then intimidation could not be ruled out. There was a need to see to implementing confidence building measures (CBMs) as well as more technical procedures for early warning and effective verification. Defence arrangements should be non-provocative. The outcome of the conference was an agreement to extend the NPT indefinitely. There was a very firm declaration that proliferation could only be tackled productively if it went beyond limitation (the superpowers had already pared down their strategic weapons by two-thirds) to that wholly essential goal, namely the completion of a Comprehensive Test Ban Treaty. Proliferation and testing were indissolubly linked.

NUCLEAR TESTING

A half-century of concern about radioactive armaments has yielded only a stop–go type of momentum. In the late 1940s there was clear disagreement in the General Assembly between mainly developing countries wanting a ban and the NWS group supporting limitation measures but unable to contemplate a complete ban. During the 1950s states were shadow-boxing with now and then a lunge or a feint, to see how far the other would give, together with some side-stepping and compromise chiefly on account of domestic pressures. Nevertheless the decade that followed, with the 1962 Cuban Missile Crisis and the radioactive contamination of the atmosphere, brought the Partial Test Ban Treaty (PTBT) to which 116 UN members affixed their signatures. Yet this treaty was not to cut out the arms race – it served only to control it. It was very much an environmental protection measure reducing fallout in the atmosphere. Underground testing continued at a significant rate. Each side worked hard to keep a lead while at the UN there was earnest talk about the need for eventual test prohibition. There were worrying indications that nuclear reduction would lead to increases in conventional strength as a counterweight. Once again, there was the grim paradox that defining arms control often leads to alternative rearming.

Sustained work by the UN Disarmament Commission and by the Conference on Disarmament was to hoist into place two measures to deal partly with nuclear consequences. An instrument for limiting US and Soviet test explosions to 150 kilotons with reciprocal verification went through in 1974 as the Threshold Test Ban Treaty (TTBT) and two years later a complementary measure dealt with the use of peaceful explosions, for instance large-scale civil engineering projects, where there was a danger of breaching the TTBT. This was the Peaceful Nuclear Explosions Treaty (PNET) of 1976.

Perhaps not surprisingly neither of the two treaties is yet in force. Defining thresholds and permitting nuclear explosions sent a message to many states (especially developing ones) that nuclear capacity or potential was a legitimate power symbol. Taken to its logical consequence, an effort to bring about complete ending of testing was surely indispensable. Scientific and public protest in the 1970s hit a vibrant note: better active today than radioactive tomorrow.

By the end of the 1980s, bipolar stand-off and state-of-the-art readiness were being replaced by regional instability. Now was the time for a broader approach, with nuclear and biological/chemical capabilities in mind, to coordinate the control possibilities of treaties and to finalise a comprehensive test ban. Expert advice to the UN was to span two approaches at the same time: that is, more expansive global policies and more specific weapons-related objectives.

The end of this century sees an encouraging consensus among formerly divided powers as to the essence of a comprehensive test ban. Major nuclear powers have imposed moratoria on their testing. The target date for UN members to have a CTB in place was the end of 1996. A number of awkward questions still stand in the way. Who is best suited to oversee control, the IAEA or a newly constituted UN agency? Would a CTB cover all possible nuclear devices from warheads to delivery systems? Could regional monitoring provide a more effective screening? How far should low-yield, simulated testing in the laboratory be allowed? This would be compensation for the ending of environmental testing but would still permit nuclear experimentation and in some quarters this is seen as scientifically questionable and by others as morally indefensible. While NWS generally support negotiations for a CTB the basic position of the United Kingdom assumes continued shelf-life for nuclear devices. A CTB is now tantalisingly near after four decades of negotiation and two and a half years of clause-by-clause drafting. An unconditional, timetabled commitment by NWS to eliminate nuclear weapons as soon as possible would clinch the treaty. In 1997 a group of twenty-eight non-aligned states propose to table a twenty-five-year programme for nuclear weapons abolition following an end to testing.

CONVENTIONAL ARMAMENTS

The contemporary world has long noted a seesaw between states relying on nuclear weapons and those which depend upon mobilised and reserve manpower. Some 80 per cent of global arms expenditure goes on conventional arms and forces and the Security Council's permanent members are the greatest spenders. At the same time, developing countries are generally incurring huge costs buying military hardware, a considerable divergence from their socio-economic needs.

The UN has not made much headway in achieving limitation of conventional armouries and personnel. The General Assembly, the Security Council, committees, commissions and Special Sessions have all issued warnings and tabled suggestions, but incantation has rarely spurred UN members into determined action. Possibilities of control are enmeshed in a web of political forces. Most ground has been won through bilateral and regional negotiation, through trade-offs between superpowers and affiliated power blocs. Predictably, the UN has inherited the old imponderable problems concerning equity, comparison and balance, problems which beset the League of Nations' disarmament workers. The old difficulties of calculating a balance between cruisers and destroyers, tanks and bomber aircraft are now translated into 'proportioning' ratios between nuclear generating forces and conventional devices. For many years no amount of urging by the UN could persuade NATO to review its nuclear reliance on containing the tank fleets and infantry hordes of the East.

Yet, already in 1973 the notion of 'mutual and balanced force reduction' (MBFR) was being explored by both NATO and the Warsaw Pact (WP). This was to prove difficult to define since reduction that way would have an impact on the size and credibility of their nuclear deterrents. To many in defence ministries downgrading nuclear options in accordance with demobilisation elsewhere would be asymmetrical and unlikely to enhance defence schemes. A way out of this dilemma was gradually worked upon by the European security body CSCE (now OSCE) doggedly contriving a set of confidence building measures (CBMs). Initially, there were polemics in Helsinki in 1975, in Belgrade through 1977–8 and in Madrid through 1980–3. Intensive UN study in diplomatic conferences and workshops brought an agreement in Stockholm in 1984 to institute a thorough surveillance system whereby parties to the pact would inform each other about manoeuvres, numbers and locations of deployed personnel and weapons, and submit to site visits and challenge inspections. In terms of firm arms control this is certainly a breakthrough and mutuality has grown with no impairment.

Also in 1984 UN protocols on conventional weapons proscribed those deemed 'excessively injurious', among them napalm and other incendiaries, cluster bombs, land-mines – all devices which could be used (for instance, as they were in Vietnam) where they did not discriminate between combatants and non-combatants.

CHEMICAL AND BIOLOGICAL WEAPONS

In this realm the UN has been vigilant and innovative. Early approaches to control of mass destruction weapons treated these two weapons systems separately, partly because expert opinion could not agree over standardising materials classified for peaceful use or hostile use. In 1972 a Convention on the Prohibition of Chemical and Biological Weapons (CBW) recruited 154 adherents. Ominously, more than a score of these states admitted to possessing chemical weapons (despite the taboo of the 1925 Geneva Protocol) and ten of them were carrying out proof-trials of biological weapons. There was every possibility that they and possibly others were undertaking quiet research into missile delivery of such devices and almost certainly looking at the possibility of radiological emission, electromagnetic impulsing, herbicides, defoliants, and even psychochemicals and genetic interference agents.

A tentative draft for on-site inspections went through the UN Conference on Disarmament in 1984 but met with vigorous opposition from the USSR who mistrusted the extent of stocks in other arsenals and, above all, the notion of open invitation to visit 'sensitive' facilities. Their suspicions seemed confirmed when that year the US Congress voted funds for a clear retaliatory capacity. Nonetheless, within eighteen months, and after intensive UN lobbying, the USSR felt reassured enough to open its laboratory doors for inspection. A CBW Protocol went to the table in New York in 1988. This obliged signatories to divulge the extent and nature of existing toxic weaponry and production facilities. Placed under UN surveillance they were to be got rid of within ten years. This time the nettle was grasped of 'dual-purpose' materials, those precursors of lethal agents which could also be seen as having a legitimate peaceful purpose. The UN was to furnish an executive council and a technical department for calculation, advice and inspection. Conference and review procedures were to be built in. Inevitably, complex questions slowed down the move for control.

Was prohibition to be fully implemented at the start or was it to be spread over a period of time? Should on-site verification be systematic, by challenge, or a combination of the two? More basically, how would a monitoring agency deal with toxic processes when defence advisers and chemical industries guard confidentiality and secrecy most closely? Would it be helpful to decentralise control to regional bodies who know their locale, as Australia and Japan have suggested? Then there was the danger of chemical terrorism (as happened recently in Japan). Would a general protocol be sensitive enough to deal with such outbreaks and conspiracies? Uncovering the nefarious intentions of the Iraqis during 1992–5 kept experts from twenty-three countries hard at work. And they had had a degree of fitful cooperation from Baghdad. A 'rolling text' of a comprehensive CBW Protocol went to the General Assembly in 1993; by April 1995, 159 had signed the Chemical Weapons Convention. A weapons ban finally came into place in October 1996 when sixty-five states had ratified the Protocol. The Convention bans the development, production, stockpiling and use of chemical weapons. A challenge inspection regime is set up to verify compliance and to monitor the industrial production of chemicals which could be used to make weapons.

ARMS TRANSFERS

Ever since the Charter was signed in 1945 the UN has been actively campaigning for limitation of arms trading or arms transfer as it is frequently termed. The contemporary scenario is both immense and elaborate: 90 per cent of arms transferred come from only six states – the USA, Russia (decreasingly), France, the UK, Italy and Germany who export particularly to the Middle East, South and East Asia, Africa and Latin America where many countries are extravagant in this respect but less so in regard to social alleviation and basic human rights.

The General Assembly frequently discusses curbing this trade but comes up against a reluctance by client states to accept restraint in the light of their inherent right to defend themselves. The suppliers are unprepared to give up dealings which fatten their exchequers and which, if displaced or terminated, would throw workers out of jobs. They seem unready to face up to what, admittedly, would be complex conversion and retraining schemes. In any case, there is always the lame rejoinder of arms dealers that 'somebody else will do it if we don't'. A difficult issue at the moment is the position of a number of East European states anxious to dispose of large redundant weapon stocks and while it is acknowledged that arms exporting facilitates militarisation elsewhere they are looking for a boost to fledgling market economies. Points such as these are met by UN suggestions that the legitimate right of defence can and should adopt a non-provocative stance. Further, defence industry conversion is practicable through schemes for decommissioning, restructuring and re-employment aided perhaps by external funding, say, from the World Bank or the European Union. Rescheduling through economic planning would shift capital and resources towards domestic, peaceful consumers.

On 9 December 1991 the General Assembly voted by a large majority to establish at the UN a universal, non-discriminatory Register of Conventional Arms. Within twelve months measures to further openness and transparency would require participants to record imports and exports of certain major offensive weapons systems and then to inform the Secretary-General. Excessive arms build-up in any one country could be identified. A UN Group of Experts is handling these procedures.

Stripping down the trade in arms is desperately slow. Dealers and their customers still throng arms fairs. National economies are in hock to defence contractors and markets. Perhaps most unhelpful of all, and the most intractable to deal with, is the politician who falls back on the principle of defensiveness-at-all-costs. The Russian delegate to the Vienna talks on stemming arms transfers put it candidly in April 1996: 'We favour', he declared, 'a reasonable degree of transparency and mutual consultation but these measures should not be detrimental to our national security interests.'

A recent event at the UN is the passing of a protocol on land-mines. There are an estimated 110 million of them spread around sixty-four countries. Each year 10,000 non-combatants (half of them children) lose their lives and thousands are maimed. Blind terrorism such as this occurs in Afghanistan, Angola, Cambodia and Madagascar. A plastic mine sold at $3 may cost a UN demining team $200 to locate and destroy and the task altogether may take another generation.

THE FIRST – AND THE LAST – WORD

If complete and overall elimination of weapons systems seems illusory what are the remaining priorities? Which avenues are worth exploring? And who are to be the trailblazers?

Those who framed the UN Charter, as we have seen, based their vision of maintained peace and security on achieving collective security. It was the ensuing arms race which brought into focus the urgency of working all-out for arms limitation. The process became confrontational arousing despair in many quarters. UN initiatives and sponsorship brought about material gains, on other occasions bipolar muscle scored the goals. It is now possible with the superpowers less hostile and, indeed, freshly agreed on the need of control and limitation that the fulcrum role of the UN can go ahead. Moreover, there is growing agreement that several improvements are desirable.

First of all, the UN could work in parallel with such regional bodies as OSCE, OAS, OAU and ASEAN. Attempts at arms control should not be duplicated. The UN has long experience of suggesting CBMs, in formulating guidelines, in mapping out programmes. There is reason to believe that some control procedures may be more effectively engineered through bilateral negotiation with the UN as an observer. Other issues, for example nuclear proliferation and testing, CBW and arms transfers, are perhaps best handled in a multilateral way. Again, more of the UN effort might be directed on narrower fronts rather than spread over the whole disarmament range. Some of these issues have already been raised earlier in this chapter. In what ways might the IAEA safeguards system be improved? Which are the urgent last phase steps to be taken to ensure the passage of a CTBT? There is the crucial problem of furnishing security assurances to less powerful states. How might this be done? With regard to arms trading, its production nature, marketing, procurement, stockpiling, registration, effective control has to move beyond rhetoric and rudimentary registration. Undoubtedly, the UN will earn greater credibility if its decision-making bodies are slimmed down, verification and investigation teams work in a more authoritative fashion, and communication and coordination between its New York headquarters and field operations is more direct. US General Omar Bradley said once that 'the search for peace is through the accumulation of peril'. The world of the twenty-first century will have to think out a more fruitful approach than that one.

6 The UN and the developing world

This chapter takes a look at what the UN has encouraged its members to do about the material betterment of a more peaceful world. First, the principles and objectives of assisted development have had to be identified and promulgated by the UN. Development Decades have been designed to translate theories into practice. There is a network of UN bodies to oversee financing and planning. Nevertheless, a good deal of earnest development work has proved disappointing; discouraging realities have led to much complacency, tortuous progress and conjecture. Finally, there is the notion of *sustainability*, something frequently seen as the absolute linchpin of rational development. As the millennium approaches there is an evident shift towards eco-politics. What are the chances today of the developing and developed worlds reaching consensus over these issues?

DISARMAMENT AND DEVELOPMENT

In absolute terms, it is said, the world must disarm if we are to live in peace. Specifically, global spending on weapons is seen as denying resources to build a fairer world community. Forty years ago, US President Eisenhower put it in these candid terms: 'Every gun that is made, every warship launched, every rocket fired signifies in a final sense a theft from those who hunger and are not fed, from those who are cold and are not clothed.' In 1980 the Brandt Commission Report (*North–South: A Programme for Survival*) put it even more graphically: 'One half of one per cent of one year's military expenditure would pay for all the farm equipment needed to increase food production and approach self-sufficiency in food-deficit low income countries by the end of the century.' More recently, there is an estimate that the $1 million spent globally each minute on arms will roughly equal the total wealth of the world by the year 2000. Measured against the task of feeding, clothing and sheltering two-thirds of the world's people this seems morally indefensible.

THE DEVELOPING WORLD

Sometimes referred to as the Third World or, rather patronisingly, as the Undeveloped World, the developing countries have a number of things in common. Perhaps 120 in number, they generally depend upon raw materials or minerals which they export to the rich world. This they have often done as colonial appendages of affluent imperial masters. Rudimentary economic strength is incapable of dealing with population pressures. Overall, seven in ten of the world's population of 5.5 billion live in disadvantaged lands. By the year 2025 there may well be a further 3 billion. It is thought that one in three of these people lives in grinding poverty and insecurity. The poorest world citizens have a mere 1 per cent of global investment and trade at their command. They are concerned not so much with the world of the future as with their next meal. The gap between their fate and expectations and those of the developed world has doubled in width over the last three decades. Even more of a challenge to any development are the gaps *within* these countries where powerful elites shift access to wealth in their favour, often endorsed by an autocratic clique in government and all at the expense of the illiterate masses in a rural hinterland. Inescapably, comparisons such as these breed resentment and conflict. Wealth and power sit impressively with forty or so UN members who account for 65 per cent of the world's gross national product. These are the launch pads for mega-enterprise which largely determine the destinies of the world's economies.

Disparities apart, it has become increasingly plain that no state in the contemporary world is self-sufficient. Poor and rich countries, Capitalist and Socialist, hang together in a mammoth economic web. The joyful prospect of self-determination put about in 1945 is today a limited one. Now no country can draw up an agenda for development in isolation. Indeed, when we use the term development it is the lives and futures of two-thirds of the world's inhabitants that we are thinking about. That must surely involve efforts for all of us.

UN DEVELOPMENT: THE PRINCIPLES

Those who drew up the UN Charter in 1945 realised only too vividly that poverty, inequality and hunger among people often lead to conflict. Early discussion in the General Assembly had in mind an international organisation encouraging economic growth and social improvement particularly for new nations groping towards self-determination. Material and moral principles come together in Charter Article 55 enjoining the UN to work for better living and employment standards, to look for solutions to interrelated social and health problems and to promote respect for human rights and basic freedoms. All UN members are pledged to joint and separate action. The emergence of new nations, the dire need of rebuilding and revitalisation after war – these were the keynotes of the development agenda.

During fifty years of dramatic global change one can discern principles being subscribed to in several ways. Action was to be in the hands of specialised agencies whose separateness the UN sought to coordinate (not always with success). Increasingly, there has been a growth in emphasis from preoccupation with accumulated growth to stepped campaigns to meet basic human needs, for instance settlement, transport, better health care, water supplies, education. By degrees, the principles put into an operational agenda have been defined and refined against the needs of emergency aid and long-term mobilisation of resources. Four elements are essential: funding aid, balance of payment support, commodity assistance, technical underpinning.

Half a century later, the principles bear the hallmark of their time when financial and trade conventions seemed immutable to many. There were few manifestations of political instability and apart from Marxist zealot cells no wide call for economic revolutions. Was it not comforting and productive to think of a process of osmosis where conferred benefit would trickle down? Of course, there were those who preferred to encourage growth from roots but in practice the 'trickle-down' rather than the 'bottom-up' approach has predominated. In some respects, this represents the elitism that is found within developing countries themselves.

UN DEVELOPMENT: THE PRACTICE

New bodies to work for development were set up in 1945 and others have emerged since then. The International Bank for Reconstruction and Development (IRBD), usually referred to as the World Bank, was to raise loan capital for major projects like factory building, railways and port enlargement. Initially, an applicant country had to prove a scheme's viability. In later years the Bank has had to cope with three big problems: the very real difficulty of some countries repaying funds, the desirability of harnessing state enterprise and private entrepreneurs, and the need to be less stringent with more than two dozen states who have become virtually bankrupt. Probably the Bank's founders never saw its brass-bound character moving into the mode of a sensitive development agency. Fiscal responsibilities are also the remit of the International Monetary Fund (IMF). The IMF has the task of helping with balance of payment difficulties or giving a kick-start to an ailing economy. Codes of conduct are drawn up, some help may be available for a country in debt, and, at least, there is consultation and expert advice.

Spearheading the UN's developmental concern is the Economic and Social Council (ECOSOC). Here fifty-four UN member states meet regularly to coordinate economic and social issues. There is close collaboration with the specialised agencies and with 600 non-governmental organisations (NGOs), all working in autonomous fashion to promote developmental awareness in the field and to build on this with schemes for material improvement, care, training and research. They operate and fashion major programmes to deal with such problems as food shortage, AIDS and drug dealing.

Two mammoth UN programmes are particularly interesting. The first is the UN Development Programme (UNDP) which is active in more than 150 countries with 6,000 projects, coordinating development schemes in almost every economic and social sector. Preliminary survey assesses the feasibility of a five-year country programme to make better use of human and natural resources, to improve living standards, and expand productivity. With ready access to the talent banks of the UN system and outside research institutes UNDP taps the most comprehensive and advanced means of technical aid available. The other programme is a more recent one originating out of the great UN environmental conference in Stockholm in 1972. Based in Nairobi, the function of the UN Environment Programme (UNEP) is to promote environmentally sound action plans for developing countries to sustain the productivity of their natural resources base including forests, water, soils and living species. Almost fifty nations have now built conservation strategies into their schemes for multifaceted development.

Lastly, it is worth noting that the UN has made special provision for decentralising development planning. Understandably, over the years there has been some concern lest planning initiatives were being kept too close to the chest of those in New York. Control out in the field is kept by Regional Commissions each exercising ECOSOC briefs in

Europe (when it was immediate postwar rebuilding), Asia and the Far East, Latin America, Africa and the Middle East. In addition, the UN Conference on Trade and Development (UNCTAD), though centred in the UN Building, in fact does much of its trade support work moving among those asking for its help with negotiation, commodity controls and marketing. In similar fashion, based in Vienna, the UN Industrial Development Organisation (UNIDO) is in the forefront of designing instruments and programmes for bringing appropriate industries to developing countries. There is a real significance in the trio of objectives shown in its mandate: promotion, acceleration, co-ordination.

THE UN DEVELOPMENT DECADES

The General Assembly in 1960 agreed that unified development planning could best be focused ('concretised') by staging approaches in successive decades. A brief look at the four Decades since 1961 enables one to judge just how development thinking is changing among UN members.

The First Decade (1961–70) was a period of boom years in the developed lands and it seemed reasonable to ask the affluent to pledge 1 per cent of their GNP to aid the poorer lands. Together, rich and poor countries would reduce the North–South gap by going for accumulated growth where economic potential was low in profile. The yearly rate of growth in developing countries was to be raised from the 1960 average of 3.5 per cent to a minimum 5 per cent in ten years. Systematic surveys of local conditions, resources (fiscal, physical and human) and specified needs would establish strategic imperatives for global planning.

During the Second Decade (1971–80) the North–South gap was yawning more widely. Among developing countries there was an obvious league table of thirty more developed countries (MDCs) and forty-five less developed countries (LDCs). Economies were soon to be wounded by an oil crisis (lasting ten years) and by rampant protectionism and sliding commodity prices. A more purposeful International Development Strategy was to have comprehensive targets, performance setting, rigorous auditing and appraisal. At the General Assembly, year after year, spokespersons for the developing countries were dissatisfied and questioning. Was it realistic to plan and operate within the scenario of the 1950s? Was it not time to do something about the way in which the rich nations kept up a dollar stranglehold, rigged and narrowed access to markets, were complacent about commodity demand and prices, and then fell back on imposed conditions and qualifications before making any real funds available? There was no fairness in having a World Bank and an IMF where decisions were taken by weighted Capitalist voting. The UN lobby of the poor nations, the so-called G77 (now it is over 120) campaigned strenuously for a New International Economic Order (NIEO). Unfair, inadequate trade and monetary regulation must be dispensed with. 'Mutually beneficial partnership' would replace one-sided dependence. A Charter of Economic Rights and Duties of States would list norms and fresh expectations. The polemic was vigorous with ideological overtones. Even so, in the years that followed the signing of the Charter in 1974 there was progress in easing trade restrictive practices. That there was little change in the fiscal area is doubtless due to the developed countries' exchequers fearing restraints upon customary practice and to the lack of decisive influence of young countries in economic affairs.

In the Third Decade (1981–90) preliminary meetings in committees and in the General Assembly heard strident complaints from countries feeling ever more disadvantaged. 'When will the developed nations give over downsizing our legitimate expectations?' asked an African trade minister in 1982. Gradually, the spotlight switched to the parlous state of LDCs and to the imperative of specific targeting of development objectives. Africa was intensively case-studied and a huge five-year revitalisation plan launched. Multinational and national teams worked in harness on blueprints and field trials stressing land reform and social betterment.

In the current Fourth Decade (1991–2000) UN members now face up to structural changes apparent everywhere like unemployment, automation, computerisation and inflation. Things like these reduce and divert resources. Investment strategies alter. Competition increases. UNIDO has begun to 'push' multifaceted programmes into Africa providing for the introduction of light industries rather than heavy industries, for small and medium-scale enterprises rather than large ones and for thorough retraining schemes. This is proving a painful process when it upsets traditional ways of living and employment. The rate of redevelopment must be rapid considering that every second three more people are born into the world, two of them in its poorest regions.

DEVELOPMENT AND UN-DEVELOPMENT: DISCOURAGING REALITIES

Is not the world's economic system structurally flawed? Asked originally in 1974 at a General Assembly, this question continues to reverberate at UN meetings. More than 100 states see themselves as liberated politically since 1945 but not at all freed from dependent, skewed, rudimentary economies. Well over half of these states stand grievously vulnerable to stagnation and inflation elsewhere. 'Are we to remain innocent bystanders and victims?' was a speculation aired also in 1974. Despite the promises of the 1974 Charter of Economic Rights and Duties developing countries are locked into volatile 'floating' exchange rates, facing resources thinned down by stringent IMF policies. Annual interest on loans and repayment charges may erode half their export earnings in some cases. There is no more credit to be had and the chill wind of recession cuts back both aid from developed states and the ability of developing states to pay their way. Political motives on all sides become suspect. Survival for many is more important than growth.

Fresh ideas are vital if the chasm between the haves and have-nots has any prospect of being narrowed. In September 1994 and after a long period of gestation the UN Secretary-General, Boutros Boutros-Ghali, issued an *Agenda for Development*. Essential components in a reassessed strategy were grassroots participation, the concept of 'self-help', the primacy of a country-by-country approach. The Secretary-General in a follow-up address to G77 ministers proclaimed a new UN mission in dramatic terms: 'We must therefore reinvent development, reinvent a new North–South social contract, reinvent a new development ethic.' He went on to point to those hindrances to fresh ideas which constrained the efforts of the UN. A mechanism for change, he believed, was 'caught in a confining cycle, caused by a resistance to multilateralism, a reluctance to provide financial means to achieve agreed aims, and an unwillingness to engage in difficult operations'. His audience was left in no doubt that they must find solutions to these problem barriers.

It is helpful, if not particularly cheering, to take a brief look at some of the issues associated with lack of development – finance, trade, energy and industrialisation. First, *finance*. Fierce criticism surrounds the World Bank's use of 'structural adjustment' schemes where, as the term suggests, a country in financial straits must pare its demands and cut back where possible to correct budget deficits. Almost certainly, this involves reining in on domestic (usually social) spending and going all out for export growth. It may make financial sense but is it not socially punishing? Cannot development policies have a human face? The work of the IMF in the field causes much resentment if it is judged that stringent demands from Washington offer no help to countries sliding inexorably into debt. Imposing an austerity programme upon a debt-defaulting country upsets the economy and if the terms of trade turn sour only the banks, foreign Capitalists and multinational corporations (MNCs), it is said, are likely to benefit.

Aid schemes from abroad, on the other hand, are gratefully received in the main but they do earn suspicion and sometimes hostility. The developed world frequently prefers bilateral aid (often conditional) between donor and recipient to the multilateral aid (unconditional) of the UN. There is less and less satisfaction among aid recipients with those schemes which impose conditions as to repayment or are given in exchange for trading advantages. Even more unacceptable are those occasions when aid is promised but is not forthcoming, when it is suspended or delayed or when it is seen as a form of sanction. The global pattern of aid indicates that aid for development is not always free from political calculation. The UK and the USA have never held to the idea of making over a consistent proportion of their GNP, instead they have preferred bilateral aid deals. Nor have they readily responded to developing countries urging swift injections of capital; rather, they have fallen back on staged programmes and the promotion of revenue-raising schemes often associated with arms programmes. They have lagged far behind the generous funding arrangements of Denmark, the Netherlands, France, Norway and Canada.

Trade in commodities like minerals or industrial raw materials is, of course, the life-blood of so many developing countries. Over the last two decades, though, market prices for coffee, cocoa and rubber have slumped disastrously. This is one of the reasons why nearly seventy countries have a debt overload of $1.9 trillion. At the same time consumer demand within those countries yearns for the attractive goods prominently featured in advertising. Revenue earned from exports may reach 85 per cent of their budgets but the crucial decisions about buying and selling are often in the hands of half a dozen MNCs. The UN has done what it can to 'roll back' hindrances to freer commerce through the painstaking intervention of the General Agreement on Tariffs and Trade (GATT) and through UNCTAD. Ironically, one consequence of liberalising trade is that countries lose their protective shields and vie with one another for survival. More positively, ingenious attempts over the past twenty years by UNCTAD have fleshed out an Integrated Programme for Commodities (IPC). For eighteen major products like bauxite, cotton, meat, sugar, tropical timber and others the creation of 'buffer stocks' aims to stabilise prices and assume dependable supplies. A Common Fund provides a cash reservoir to pay for stocking and distribution.

Next to finance, *energy* questions excite most controversy at UN meetings. The growth of dependency on imported forms of energy is comparatively recent. Self-sufficiency has given way to crucial links between suppliers and consumers. It needs only interruption of supplies or contest over their source to raise political tensions into crisis. The UN is grappling with three aspects of energy use: scarcity, waste, pollution. It is estimated that by 2020 the world's consumption of energy from all types of fuel will at least have doubled. There are finite limits to reserves of coal, oil and even water power and there are political barriers to exploitation. Thus, a number of specialised agencies have in hand both conservation policies for existing stocks and research into alternatives such as solar and wind power and the possibilities of geothermal and biomass conversion. As for waste, why is it that Japan uses only half the energy per unit of industrial production that the United States does? How far is it possible to prevent the gross misuse of precious energy sources in poorer countries? It is considered in regard to pollution that incentives secure better responsible use than sanctions.

Industrialisation is often thought of as the crock of gold at the foot of the developing rainbow. That was the route the developed world followed. Why should two-thirds of the world's people account for only 9 per cent of the world's industry? Debate about these issues has frequently become strident at conferences and workshops convened by the UN. Denied for years the resources to mechanise and diversify, countries now crave an opportunity to construct something tangible. Elsewhere, there is the spectacular economic miracle of certain formerly dependent territories – Hong Kong, Taiwan, Singapore and South Korea. Are there not corners to be cut? Growth in wealth and an explosion in living standards has climbed exponentially in those places. For most other developing countries the reality of prospects for an industrial new era is a distinctly sobering one. Although heads have nodded in assent at the often-heard UN precept that industrialisation is 'the crucial engine and catalyst of developed progress', there is little evidence that detailed blueprints and decision exist in areas ripe for expansion. There is no escaping the fact that the trading practices of richer industrialised countries not only discourage technological extension but tend to benefit the rich since the technologies have to be imported from them. When transported without being adapted to the needs and conditions of a developing country these technologies can lead to even more dependence for maintenance and growth. Availability of cheap labour is no longer a key to economic transformation. What is wanted, as the developed countries are finding, is a pool of 'flexible' labour capable of redeployment and retraining. How does this square with the obvious difficulty of funding capital-intensive production? If endemic poverty (born of large and ever-increasing numbers) is the severest problem would not the best solution be to go for job creation? That may not accord with the preferences of the World Bank, the IMF, or of entrepreneurs, for 'lean management'. In practice, however, it makes more sense not to follow the fashion of building large-scale plants but rather to promote modest-sized enterprise. This is the alternative approach – the 'small is beautiful' approach of E. F. Schumacher and his followers, with their insistence on 'economics as if people mattered'.

SUSTAINABILITY

The roots of what we now term sustainable development were visible at the UN Stockholm Conference in 1972. There, 113 states agreed that it was vital to manage developing growth so that resources were not over-exploited and did not endanger the ability of future generations to meet their own needs. The future must never be sacrificed on account of a short-term dash for short-term gains. This truth contains a paradox in that sustained momentum, a lack of restraint, will be suicidal. Tough questions then arise for both developed and developing countries. In the first case, how are developing countries to be persuaded to conserve and enhance their resource base? Perhaps by going slowly? This, however, would make even wider the gap between the haves and the have-nots. Is it possible to convince less developed countries that they must shift the nature of development to one less material and energy intensive? These issues arouse and sometimes inflame anxiety in countries in the disadvantaged South. The dangers of environmental degradation resulting from unregulated development are acknowledged. To go hell-bent for incremental growth is to invite disaster. In their eyes, however, the most toxic effect on the environment is poverty. If rational management then lessens the move to aggregate growth how do they procure resources and build wealth to deal with that poverty?

Problems associated with 'going for growth' were illumined in the report of the Brundtland Commission (the World Commission on Environment and Development) in 1987. The report, *Our Common Future*, argues powerfully for a closer partnership between industrialised and developing countries. For the latter, 'revived growth' must be of a new kind in which sustainability, equity, social justice and security are firmly embedded as major social goals alongside environmental and economic goals. Planning and programming along these lines require a higher level of commitment by all countries to the satisfactory working of multilateral institutions and much more careful and more constructive dialogue and negotiations.

In 1992, 178 states met in Rio de Janeiro at a UN Earth Summit. Environment and development were seen to be interrelated. Accountability, carefully managed change and clear incentives would steer change – sustainably. In the course of a vibrant dialogue eco-development soon became eco-politics. It was the affluent who were most worried about spoiling the biosphere. They were even suggesting that loans be granted only if the applicant could prove environmental viability. Sanctions might be levied against those who were developing 'irresponsibly'. A Rio Declaration roundly stated that in order to achieve sustainable development, environmental protection should constitute 'an integral part of the development process'. This soon brought forth the rejoinder from poorer states who felt at risk that, 'Unless developing countries have true [that is, unconditional] access to ecologically sound technology they cannot be expected to make the transition to sustainable development.' There seemed to be a plaintive stress on the point of 'access'. Appeals from the platform for environmentally friendly partnership between richer and poorer states actually brought a taunt of 'eco-colonialism' from some frustrated delegates.

The position several years after Rio appears to be that while the majority of countries accept the frequently proclaimed tenets of sustainability and would like to see them realised they do not quite see how the precepts are to become operable in the near future given the constraints of their own poor leverage and the likely restraints, qualifications and evasions that vested interests (mainly among the rich) are likely to resort to. However, much development is scheduled to turn green. Even so, one question begs an answer. Who is to co-ordinate development initiatives? Is there anyone in an overall position legitimately able to convene discussions among 185 states and hundreds of NGOs, to carry through exhaustive studies, and to put into being intensive 'PR' to build consensus? Has anyone other than the UN the experience of half a century's thought and planning? Mistakes have been made and will be made but with the UN as fulcrum, development policies are more likely to be 'global politics in the human interest'.

7 The UN and an urbanising world

This chapter considers the contemporary world as an urbanising world. Our world is now made up increasingly of towns. By the year 2000 every second person in the world will live in a town. Eight out of ten of them will live in what we now term the developing world. Globally, the world is urbanising at the rate of 250,000 each day. In the first decade of the next century nine out of ten of the world's largest cities will be in Africa or Asia or Latin America – cities such as Lagos, Beijing and Sao Paulo. These will be *megacities*. Forty-five years ago there were 100 cities exceeding 1 million in size; in 2010 there will be 1,000, of the same size, half of them planned by the present government of China. Thus, the contemporary world is steadily fragmenting into tight overloaded knots of people, all competing for shelter, jobs and decent living standards. Lack of housing, fresh water and sanitation has been estimated by the WHO as already responsible for many millions of deaths, perhaps half of them children. The WHO, again, believes that in London and New York the homeless in the streets have a life expectancy more than twenty-five years lower than the national average. If the urbanising world has its problems of congestion, decline, confusion, crime and alienation, its magnetism impacts upon surrounding rural areas. In many respects this world of urbanisation is as potent a threat to a reasonable human habitat, indeed to survival itself, as environmental collapse in the natural world.

URBANISING ENTERS THE UN AGENDA

The previous chapter discussed how UN member states have shaped up to a responsibility conferred by the 1945 Charter – that of helping new nations achieve growth, social health and political self-determination. Conventionally, then and since, we have distinguished the *developing* and the *developed* worlds, each offering more or less sophisticated and agreeable environments. That distinction is no longer true of the contemporary world. In the sense of coming to terms with revolutionary changes in industry, population growth and movements, social mores, expectations and communications all states are developing. They are encountering similar problems, perhaps the greatest of which is the spread of urban environments at the expense of almost everything else. The geography of advantage and disadvantage, it has been said, is a thing of the past. There seems to be an imperative need to search collectively for solutions to shared problems.

For over twenty-five years UN members have come together to see what might be done about urbanisation. The first great conference on human settlements was in May–June 1976 in Vancouver. Termed Habitat I, it was preceded by preparatory commissions in Teheran, Cairo and Caracas. Altogether, delegates from 134 states attended, as did 250 NGOs. To begin with, there was a Declaration of Principles setting out the need of rapid and continuous improvement of the quality of life (so it was termed) with priority given to the needs of the least well-off. Disparities between urban and rural settlements were to be reduced. Recommendations for national action followed. Principles, it was urged, only see life if planning promotes and guides development rather than relying on basic control and restriction. Correspondingly, urban development must take effect through strategies that assess needs in regard to shelter, infrastructure and services. Public and private finance and construction sectors had to work in harness. In outline these recommendations seem reasonable enough yet they were to bring to the surface differences among politicians, economists and planners. Guidance, it was pointed out, might be acceptable both to the professional and the layman; however, the realisation of the desirable was often frustrated and negated by commercial forces. In how many countries, for instance, could land be regarded as a public resource when all too often it was treated as a market commodity, an instrument of financial speculation? It was the existence of un-public land that led representatives of the developing world, the Group of 77, to deplore their 'bifurcated urban society' where a small minority enjoyed superior space and an imported and exotic level of comfort while the mass squatted elsewhere. The delegates from industrial nations echoed the tune. What Los Angeles and Liverpool had done unhappily twenty-five years ago Bombay, Shanghai and Accra were doing today. Who, then, would ever 'control' the motivation of some civic heads and town planners in new countries to bid for erecting the magic symbols of freeways, vast shopping malls and luxury hotels enticing visitors while doing little for cramped urban crowds?

There was general agreement at Vancouver on two points. In the first place urbanisation, in itself, was not necessarily bad. Urban problems were largely the result of bad management. Countries must learn together and act together. Then, there were warnings that the cyclical nature of urban boom and decay must be reckoned with. From time to time more people were leaving than entering Calcutta, Rio de Janeiro or Mexico City.

It was to be expected that Habitat I would earn some criticism. Was it not wildly optimistic? Others in those Cold War days pointed to the political wrangling which often aborted consensus. Nevertheless, sixty-four recommendations to governments called for specific changes. And understanding was growing among politicians and planners that the urbanising world was a poverty-stricken one where rights and duties so grandly spoken of in the UN Charter would depend upon determined efforts to bring about straightforward material betterment. It was the voluntary and community group sector in many countries that heard the warning bell and then began to put heads together.

There was a big step forward in 1978. That year the General Assembly set up the United Nations Centre for Human Settlements (UNCHS) to assist individual countries and the world community to manage urbanisation. Located in Nairobi it was to be a think-tank and a service centre. Operating principles were fairly plain. Human settlements were to be understood as 'the physical articulation of the social, economic and political interaction of people living in communities'. Urban development then transformed a natural environment into a concentrated, built one with interlocked components such as shelter, transport, place of employment, social services, recreation and the institutions to produce and manage them. With shelter as an all-out priority UNCHS drew up a Global Strategy for Shelter to the Year 2000 to coordinate efforts to facilitate provision. Almost twenty years later this appears to have been an adventurous goal.

UNCHS went on to initiate several comprehensive programmes which are still ongoing today. The Sustainable Cities Programme, based on the belief that cities are short of management capacity rather than capital, aims to develop 'eco-sensitive' management skills among civic planners; the Localising Agenda Programme seeks to encourage joint ventures between local authorities, the private sector and community groups; the Settlement Infrastructure and

Environmental Programme supports the action plans of poorer countries in furnishing basic services; an Indicators Programme is an ambitious experiment in data-banking the actions that are under way in urban locales worldwide.

URBANISATION ON TODAY'S UN AGENDA

Despite two decades of effort and patchwork progress, rapid urbanisation has outstripped the capacity of governments to provide housing and fair living conditions for great masses of people. The UN decided to put in hand preparations for another conference on human settlement, this time scheduled for Istanbul and June 1996. There were three main themes, namely adequate shelter for all people as soon as practicable, sustainable settlement in an urban world, and partnership as a vital base for management progress (i.e. governments, local authorities and NGOs). Localised approaches were to be stressed: Habitat I had seemed far too general in its approaches. The themes were to be handled in two ways: first, the general recommendations from Habitat I would be made more specific and, second, there would be a thorough review of Agenda 21, the wide-ranging action plan adopted at the UN meeting on the environment and development, UNCED, held in Rio in 1992, the so-called Earth Summit. Throughout the proceedings there would be particular attention to the needs of women and society's vulnerable groups whose life chances were so markedly restricted by inequality and marginalisation. Istanbul was determined to put its best foot forward in the light of years of complacency and uncoordinated efforts.

The Vancouver principles were reiterated rather more purposefully at Istanbul. Decision was to move through stated principles to specific commitments and then to a global plan of action. Despite its name, the global plan focused not so much on global schemes as on developing strategies, applicable to cities and towns worldwide, taking local characteristics into account. The timescale for the enterprise was to be two decades, with special emphasis on remedial action. Guidelines for urban renewal were supplied to conference delegates. Policies were to be shaped appropriate to the local situation, not to be imported models or ideologies. In response to this point, there set out for Istanbul strong delegations of local authority administrators particularly from the United States, the United Kingdom and from Council of Europe member states. The best way forward was to strengthen institutional structures. Women should always be involved. Not everything could be left to the market. Democratic collaboration would recruit capital and talents and at the same time attack constraints particularly in finance and land. There had to be 'transparency' of intention and accountability with no leaden bureaucracy.

In two respects Habitat II blazes new trails. First, holistically, it is the culmination of a series of major UN conferences – on social development, women, population, the environment. And because half of us in the next century will live in cities the City Summit of 1996 expects action on most of the recommendations agreed at those earlier conferences. Second, there was an expectation at the UN that here was a new kind of conference. It was a big event with 13,000 delegates from 184 states but in its makeup and proceedings the accent was on working groups and detailed, accurate note-taking. Habitat II was a sterner experience than Vancouver. Much-thumbed conference documentation like the *Global Report on Human Settlements 1996* and the *Human Development Report 1995* put the situation squarely and starkly. Massive urbanisation is the only way the world can survive its massive population surges. Urban areas afford higher life expectancy, lower absolute poverty, more effective use of resources, easier access to health care and education, lower costs per household for basic services and waste disposal. These survey findings, bold on the printed page, were not the experience of all delegates. There was debate and dissension. Consensus, though, was reached on the point that poor management, failing to enlist the talents and knowledge of the local community, leads to towns becoming the victims of haphazard, unhealthy development.

'How do we best illustrate what we think is necessary and desirable?' was a question asked by participants in Istanbul. Fortunately, the UN seems to have anticipated this need and, six months earlier in Dubai, had convened a conference on Best Practices in Improving Living Environments. Was it not possible to identify cities and towns around the world which had realised successful and sustainable solutions to urbanisation? Criteria for 'best practice' ranged over attainment of tangible improvements in such things as adequate housing, local transport, essential services and amenities. These were measured against key Habitat II themes – *engagement*, involving people, *sustainability*, ensuring today's resource use does not disadvantage the next generation, and *equity*, provision of opportunities for popular participation in decision. Some of the 'best practices' make interesting reading. For instance, in 1970, Chattanooga, Tennessee, was one of the most polluted US cities, declining and decaying. Over some twenty-three years a determined group of government officials, business and community groups was able to clean up the locale and revitalise the economy. Factories were regrouped in a 'zero emissions industrial park', wastelands were cleared and reused, affordable housing created. Economic and environmental development benefited. Then in Brazil, Curitiba has coordinated five diverse rejuvenation projects. City transport has been rejigged, there is resourceful twinning of waste management schemes and job creation, an imaginative designing of water and parkland facilities and a network of information technology library facilities for schools and for the public. Curitiba is different in the words of its architect teamleader. It has 'gone against the flow and made itself a human city. Every city could do the same.' Another example is Dubai in the United Arab Emirates. This is a city which has mushroomed from 50,000 people forty-five years ago to its present 700,000. Urban management techniques have been most carefully applied with a 'bottom-up' approach which features collaboration between public and private sectors and local community representatives, especially from women's groups. This enterprise is certainly in contrast to those towns in the Middle East and around the Mediterranean which have peppered their townscapes with prestige high-rise buildings.

The rhetoric at Habitat II was impressive, the debate keen and large scale. Nevertheless, according to the UN Secretary-General, who was there, there are many hard questions to answer. For example, what are the best means of financing urban improvement? Can we be sure by a target date that satisfactory shelter will be available for all? What schemes are most effective for combating poverty in run-down areas? How far is it possible to ensure basic hygienic betterment in urban areas without causing long-term damage to the natural environment? In what ways can the cycle of depression, conflict, devastation and failure to develop, so obvious in many modern towns, be broken? An inevitable conclusion struck Dr N'Dow, the Secretary-General of Habitat II. Urbanisation was not the cause of so many city problems, rather it was like a mirror reflecting them, 'a microcosm in which, paradoxically, they are magnified'. 'We cannot stop the process of urbanisation', he said. Nor should we. 'It is at the heart of a new world in the making. It is, in many ways in fact, the engine driving it.'

CONCERN LEADS TO CONTROVERSIES

Debate at Habitat II stirred controversies which have constant resonance in many other places. Today's world is richer than it was in 1950. World income has grown from $4 trillion to $23 trillion and in per capita terms income has trebled. Towns have more resources; they have a right to grow. There is a dilemma here for the poorest countries. How will they fill their exchequers, improve their balance of trade, enrich their people if they neglect urban development? Many of these countries, deep in debt, have been forced to accept and apply 'structural adjustment policies' imposed by the IMF. These measures have certainly increased urban poverty. It is proving very difficult for the poor and needy in such countries to reject continued economic growth even though outside experts shake their heads over its challenge to 'sustainability'. Towns must expand opportunities. The modern world faces a huge job shortage. The UN has estimated that there are 35 million job seekers in industrial countries. In newer lands there could be a need for 1 billion new jobs during the next ten years. It is the town that offers employment chances of a new variety for in industrial countries 66 per cent are employed in the service sector and in Africa and Asia 25 per cent. We also have what one might term differences in urban dynamic. Surveys made for Habitat II illustrate the well-known fact that while some urban centres thrive others stagnate. There are functional reasons for this – towns may be administrative, market, or industrial, or tourist centres. There are dormitory satellites and the booming complexes in Silicon Valleys. The megacity has an ethnic mix (sometimes ghettos) and established quarters with acknowledged social connotations. No longer can it be said that 'developing' and 'developed' countries are altogether different in the degree or nature of urbanisation. In many respects the countries that are still relatively poor have covered as much distance in twenty years in urbanising terms as did the industrial world in a century. The result is not a happy or healthy one. On the other hand, as the UN surveys reveal, a number of countries with low incomes have tried hard to improve living prospects for their urban population. Countries in this category are Cyprus, Barbados, Madagascar and Costa Rica and they stand out against countries, rich in resources, which neglect their urban settlements, like Nigeria, Brazil and South Africa.

An issue that continues to arouse vigorous discussion as we have seen it did at Habitat II is that of concentration versus decentralisation. This is sometimes seen as 'grey' thinking versus 'green' thinking. The former position argues that concentration reduces environmental impact and more effectively concentrates services and amenities in an area serving (from a supply point of view) an optimum number of people. Building on this scale, it is said, maintains efficiency and comfort and makes enhancement practicable. The contrary argument to this is equally strong. A 'green' necessity in urban development prefers dispersal to reduce impact on environment. The actual urban superstructure required per resident goes up radically as the size of a town increases beyond a certain point. The smaller community has a dynamic that is essentially stimulating and pleasurable: in the large agglomeration the resident is soon encountering isolation. These points about urbanisation appear to be incompatible. Certainly, within the UN both points of view have their adherents.

Another issue much discussed is the obvious liking by UN experts and personnel for public participation in urban planning and schemes for regeneration. The desirability of this was prominently voiced at both Habitat I and Habitat II, more loudly on the second occasion. Popular participation in urban planning is fine in theory and worth encouraging. It may be practicable in those places where seven out of ten of the world's people are fortunate to live under pluralistic and democratic regimes. What is likely to happen elsewhere? When the 'man in the street' is listened to is it sometimes anything other than perfunctory consultation with groups who are merely invited to comment on proposals prepared by small teams of professionals? That might be democratic but it does not look like participation as the settlement conferences saw it. In the United Kingdom the Department of the Environment has made it known that while the layman's lack of expertise is granted there is a clear value in encouraging a wider degree of consultation before blueprints are drawn up. The development process may gain in urgency, misunderstandings and conflicts can be resolved. Community regeneration (this is a government declaration) requires a new understanding of urban 'wealth' to do with evaluation of *all* its resources – social, economic, cultural, environmental.

IS AN URBANISING WORLD A DEHUMANISING WORLD?

Almost sixty years ago Louis Mumford, an American sociologist, wrote a powerful study, *The Culture of Cities*, which has been read widely. He believed that in all countries the city was suffering a cultural, social and economic mutation from a vibrant social institution into an 'insensate industrial town'. It was 'Coketown, a barbaric factory slum, ruined by the shapeless giantism of megalopolis'. He thought, however, that with careful planning, humane as well as business-like, the urban habitat could be remodelled perhaps with 'polynucleated settlements' where individuals and groups would be living in satellite centres rather than in a central, amorphous core.

Similar ideas abound today. Contemporary agglomeration, the thrust of urbanisation, poses inescapable problems for all the world's peoples. The problems can be addressed step by step as the UN's Habitat I and Habitat II have shown but only if there is a good measure of collective and radical determination. Survival is in the balance as the Secretary-General of Habitat II warned delegates:

> if we want to save the future we have no choice other than to find answers today to one of the most neglected and urgent problems of our time, one that goes to the very heart of our everyday lives – how we live, where we live, and, above all, if we live at all.

8 Helping refugees

The world of 1945, recovering from a world war, framed the UN Charter in a burst of idealism and optimism. Things would be put right eventually as a collective will went into operation. The contemporary world is dramatically different, torn by discrimination and marred by displacement. Millions march, ousted and victimised. The world terms them 'refugees'. They have no home, no job, no money, no rights, no hope. They have no settled home. They are looking for an asylum, a place to settle as the beginning of peace. There are many of them – the latest UN estimate (a rough and ready one) speaks of no less than 18 million asylum seekers and refugees and well over 25 million people internally displaced within countries. The contemporary world is the world of the Great Unwanted. What can the UN do to help them? This chapter will take a good look at the problem of refugees.

THE REFUGEE AS AN INTERNATIONAL PROBLEM

The refugee of today's world is not a new figure. The Bible presents the search of a chosen people for a home to call their own. Over the centuries people have fled from individual harrying or from despotic rule to places such as Britain or the United States. After the First World War the League of Nations had to feed and shelter hundreds of thousands in eastern Europe as revolutions toppled dynasties. Nazi persecution in the 1930s sent large numbers of Austrians and Czechs abroad. And after the Second World War Europe was flooded with 'displaced persons' ('DPs') and prisoners of war – 21 million of them.

As an emergency measure in 1945 to cope with what was thought to be a temporary period of crisis and chaos the UN hastily commissioned an International Refugee Organisation (IRO) as a field agency to work with local authorities and volunteers from many lands. It was realised quite soon that this was an inadequate stopgap. Member states must share the burden and costs of resuscitating a broken continent. First-aid measures from soup kitchens to tented camps gave some possibility of future life to gaunt skeletons from concentration camps and to whole families swept from their homelands. When they were fit to travel many were aided to emigrate to Britain, Israel, Canada and the United States. Added to their physical distress, moreover, was the suspicion of some receiving authorities that a victim might be a 'fellow-traveller' of Nazi or Communist inclination. In those days brotherhood frequently acquired a political colouring.

From the very beginning of its existence the UN has recognised the task of caring for the displaced as a matter of concern in accordance with the Charter. Accordingly, in January 1957, the United Nations High Commission for Refugees (UNHCR) was set up, first as a sub-organisation of the General Assembly, later as a specialised agency. With headquarters in Geneva and supported then by eighty states, its function was to provide protection and material relief, and to search for a lasting solution to homelessness. Such tasks were to be approached through negotiation with governments. There was no indication then that UNHCR would ultimately be working hands-on, as it were, in the field.

THE REFUGEE DEFINED

Strict definition is essential as we shall presently discover. In the eyes of UNHCR a refugee is:

> any person who owing to a well-founded fear of being persecuted for reasons of race, religion or nationality, or public opinion, is outside the country of his nationality and is unable or, owing to such fear, unwilling to avail himself of the protection of that country.

This definition is still held to whenever possible. A Convention on the Status of Refugees in 1951 fleshed out the definition when it attempted to enumerate the rights and duties of the refugee, among other things the right to protection and the duty to observe the law in a host state. Even so this convention still has been ratified by fewer than half the UN's member states. Some years later, in 1967, a follow-up protocol set out the obligations and responsibilities of states ratifying it and laid down basic requirements as to freedom of movement for the refugee, assurances about employee status, public health and education. A vital safeguard built into this protocol, eventually to be signed by 110 states, was the main principle of *non-refoulement* which prohibited the expulsion or forcible return of a person to a country where he or she might have cause to fear persecution.

UN HELP FOR REFUGEES

Bearing in mind the definition set out above and the principle of no return there are four main approaches UNHCR adopts in its care for the refugee: emergency relief, voluntary repatriation, asylum reception, and resettlement.

Emergency relief supplies of basic essentials to survival such as food, shelter and medical aid have been sent to many areas of persecution in Africa, Asia, the Middle East and Latin America. A comprehensive operation requires an airlift, delivery by road, warehousing and distribution. Where possible the enterprise must be kept in the hands of civilian staff although they may need armed escorts. Many instances of these mercy missions have been spectacularly successful in saving lives where there has been dogged collaboration between UNHCR and NGOs such as *Médecin sans Frontières*, the Save the Children Fund, Oxfam, the Society of Friends and other religious groups. There is a twilight existence for the recipients and for the relief staff and the drip-feed of relief needs medical and nutritional monitoring. The goal must therefore be food security through the attainment of food self-sufficiency. Nevertheless, in these circumstances how long will the life-support machine of relief be required to operate in any location? Moreover, in what respects does an external agency move through emergency aid to guaranteed long-term support?

Voluntary repatriation is a return to place of origin as soon as conditions have improved and safety is assured. Individuals may be helped with travel and subsistence; elsewhere, large-scale transport of groups may be needed. Governments must be approached about admission. Problems are many. How can the UN depend upon a government which grants an amnesty or some other form of guarantee? Is it practicable for an outsider like the UN to go on maintaining help for near-destitute and barely tolerated people after their readmission to a state which should be caring for them? Will a state receiving repatriates be willing to reabsorb those who need housing, transport, employment when such things are in short supply for those who stayed (perhaps without protest)? The plan for relocating Moslems in Bosnia has been seen by some as underpinning the loathsome 'ethnic cleansing' strategy of Bosnian Serbs. In parts of Africa and

Asia UNHCR acknowledges that the repatriate needs the kinship bonds of an extended family which traditionally shelters the vulnerable person in hard times. Without this no 'returnee' can be other than bereft.

Asylum reception is the long-term processes of facilitating shelter and eventual integration within a host community. Everything depends upon the immigration policies of admitting states. Often, only a specific quota is granted shelter. Priority may be given to 'vulnerable' refugees such as women and children or the handicapped. In the country of first or second asylum a state has to check the applicant's status, to provide for basic needs, to unite a family where possible, to help an individual earn a living, and, one day, either settle as a naturalised citizen or be encouraged to return. International law in the Universal Declaration of Human Rights of 1948 and in the Convention on the Status of Refugees provides only for the right to *seek* asylum and not the right to be granted asylum. This has become clear in recent years when a number of European states have become niggardly in granting visas to those they see as 'abusive' applicants. Germany, Sweden, Switzerland were liberal and hospitable to begin with but, along with Britain, then became less so. The 'failed asylum seeker' has become a pathetic figure in the contemporary world. Some of them, fruitlessly travelling in search of shelter, have been termed 'refugees in orbit'.

Resettlement, ideally, helps refugees to help themselves towards self-sufficiency. If the refugee is unable or unwilling to be repatriated then resettlement elsewhere is a hoped-for solution. A number of Secretary-Generals have been successful in persuading governments to offer homes to political refugees. China has been ready to absorb 250,000 Vietnamese workers in its state farms and fisheries. Tanzania, Zaire and Pakistan have accepted large numbers of those fleeing despotism. Such reception is generally in the country of 'first asylum'. What happens, though, if UNHCR manages to get refugees resettled in their original country of residence? Are these people on return to their villages then free from discrimination and harassing? In Cambodia the United Nations Transitional Authority (UNTAC) brought back 370,000 people to their ricelands still in the shadow of their former fearsome enemy, the Khmer Rouge. For how long and in what manner can the UN protect these 'fresh starters', traumatised by war, many of them disabled by wandering through minefields?

Integration, wherever it is scheduled to take place, demands the learning of a new language, traditions and cultural values. Resettlers are hanging on and hanging in. At one level, the most successful example of resettlement is probably that of the Jews who fled postwar Europe for Palestine which then became Israel in 1948. As citizens of a new state they ceased to be refugees. Nonetheless, their neighbours, the Palestinian Arabs, then became refugees languishing in desert camps, some of them for two generations. It was resettlement for some, the wilderness for others.

THE REFUGEE AND THE MIGRANT

In the early days of the UN it was not too difficult to identify those who were suffering from persecution. As the years rolled on people in Africa and Asia were being displaced by the thousands and then by the million. Soon there were 10,000 each day in need of assistance. The General Assembly of the UN recommended a more flexible interpretation of the UNHCR criteria. Areas of conflict were spotlighted where relief and protection must be hurried in to uprooted groups for whom individual definitions of refugee status were impracticable.

The displaced and dispossessed have for half a century made up a jigsaw pattern in the contemporary world. In the 1940s and 1950s there were Europe's 'DPs' and Palestinian Arabs. Twenty years later, in the 1960s and 1970s, many thousands fled from volatile upheavals in Africa and South East Asia as crumbling imperial colonies were replaced by new, often faction-ridden, nations. Over the last twenty years the world has witnessed a host of conflict and genocidal missions displace millions at gunpoint in former Yugoslavia, Cambodia, Haiti, Iraq, Burma, Rwanda, Georgia, Chechnya, Lebanon, Liberia and Mozambique. The most hospitable countries often taking thousands of the hapless have been the Scandinavian lands, Germany, Austria, Switzerland, Pakistan, Iran, Tanzania, Uganda and Malaysia, often at some sacrifice.

A further complication to a watertight definition has steadily become evident. There are those, by the hundred thousand, who escape by the skin of their teeth a civil conflict, an earthquake or a flood and then clamber into some leaky craft or hastily purchased aircraft seat. Many find themselves pawns of push–pull economic forces. These are the economic migrants desperate to move out in search of any life opportunity elsewhere. Is a caring world to deny them refuge in the widest sense of that term? Seven out of ten of them come from countries with poor human rights records. The UN meets dilemmas here. Protest from New York is seen as interference by sovereign states. A clampdown by an offending state makes it more difficult for relief to gain access. If UNHCR launches large-scale transit arrangements the result may be a flood of migrants knocking on the doors of more fortunate lands asking for sanctuary. Spasms of public concern often encourage governments to be more liberal but all too often a state withdraws into a fortress introducing stricter visa regulations, more stringent border controls, waiting periods and even detention and expulsion of the unfortunate. Very little is being done by some UN members to work out management techniques that are both effective and charitable. There is much 'short-termism' looking the other way, or the knee-jerk assertion that the boat is already overcrowded. Aside from prejudice and complacency there is the consequence of growing numbers and confused decision known as 'compassion fatigue'.

Another victim of displacement is the environmental migrant. For centuries people have fled from an inhospitable earth in the wake of flood, landslip, earthquake, lava flow, invading desert. Some of these movements are relatively simple responses to conditions which worsen (often dramatically so), others may be more complex adjustments to the social deterioration of less good living space. It is no coincidence that the lands prominently featured in any list of the producers of environmental migrants are experiencing ecological disasters and are often galvanised by armed conflicts, as is the case in Sudan, Chad, Afghanistan, Haiti, Honduras and Ethiopia. Now, perhaps, there is another prospect of mass migration dawning: the irreversible destructive potential of rising sea levels caused by global warming which would inundate crowded delta regions in Africa and Asia.

Ironically, development schemes, generally considered a force for good, may lead to displacement. Dams and irrigation projects, it is said, have uprooted 26 million villagers in parts of India. It has never been easy for the UN to remonstrate, say, with a government or commercial undertaking which is 'going for gold' without taking the human consequences into account. Environmental concerns, too much 'Greenwatching', are seen by many national governments as getting in the way of resource exploitation.

Put briefly, UN member states are going to have to take an urgent look at UN mandates for dealing with migration both of the persecuted and of the opportunistic. Earlier definitions cannot address mass flight and complexity of motive. Clear lines of action will be vital. Protection and rescue of legitimate political refugees primarily depends on diplomatic negotiation with governments. Strategies to handle economic and environmental migrants (many will be both) could benefit from some early warning system, and then international plans for assistance, possible compensation, and careful, safeguarded long-term resettlement. Can anything less than this be done? And who else would do it than the international collective of the UN?

THE UN AND STANCHING THE FLOW

To a much greater extent than could have been foreseen at its inception UNHCR has become a working agency in the field. Half of its total budget goes to fund relief in Africa. There are forty-seven African states adhering to the Convention of 1951 and the Protocol of 1967 and six of them have produced major population outflows. More than 5 million afflicted victims have trekked across Angola, Liberia, Ethiopia, Sudan and Somalia, strafed by rival warlords. Farmers have laid siege to cities, the more fortunate have emplaned for Sweden or the Netherlands. There is a 'brain drain' too with more Ethiopian doctors in the United States than in the homeland. Debt, inflation, drought beggar those who remain behind. Out of the confusion some useful schemes have emerged. A series of international meetings in the last ten years have brainstormed possible remediation and multinational teams are at work in the worst-hit areas. African governments have not lacked resolve. Tanzania sees to the separate integration of urban migrants and rural migrants, skill-training the former and using cooperative, land-reform plans for the latter. Mozambique was faced with the absorption of 1.5 million people displaced from six neighbouring lands. UNHCR and other specialised agencies spearheaded resettlement schemes in an area twice the size of Germany that were to last three years and cost $200 million.

Asian countries have encountered the problem of the 'refusee', those who stay in transit camps hoping that policies back home may change. Some 62,000 Vietnamese have refused shelter at home and sailed dangerously for Hong Kong, or Singapore or Japan. This, of course, strains patience and resources in countries of first asylum. Negotiations between UNHCR and Vietnam have shaped a Comprehensive Plan of Action funded by seventy-six UN member states. All who have left are screened to determine their motives and they are given a choice between staying in crowded transit camps or returning to Vietnam under UNHCR protection. The 'returnees', half under the age of 15, are given grants and some assistance with housing to enable them to work and settle. It will be obvious that an external agency such as UNHCR has to tread political minefields. There is a fine line to be drawn between those moral principles which level condemnation at offending states and the actual pragmatic need to work with the offenders and with a variety of 'rogue' states if any deliverance is to be effected. There will always be the danger that the neutrality of the UN is misunderstood or mishandled. Always there is the charge, particularly in Latin America and in the Middle East, that UNHCR intercession is troublesome interference. It is not unknown in those regions for political dissidents to refuse identification and help from outside; it may be safer to stay at home and lie low. Particularly in those countries, given the nature and number of oppressive regimes there may be nowhere else to go that is dependable.

OLD PROBLEMS, NEW APPROACHES

For the UN the continuity of care is unceasing. Great things have been done. Yet, with twenty migrants today for every one in 1945, the stanching of flows looks like spiralling out of control. It seems imperative now for the UN to think afresh. What seem to be the main issues? First, perhaps, the definitions should be scrutinised. A well-founded fear of persecution has enlarged into a well-founded fear of dispossession and displacement. Numbers may justify broader terms of concern and a more forceful mandate. The danger is that the status of the original 'person of concern', the political refugee, becomes clouded and swamped. There is a need now for UN members to take action on several fronts. After all, they reaffirmed those Charter principles of the 'dignity and worth of the human person' and the practice of tolerance. They must declare that they will take steps to eliminate human rights violation. They should offer security assurances to minorities and to the marginalised in their lands. They must join others in working out a strategy to deal with *all* types of migrants. It will be a tremendous task for the UN to persuade governments to harmonise liberal asylum principles and legitimate immigration policies. They cannot show the door much longer to large swathes of the human race.

Second, there is the matter of what might be termed preventive intervention. If definitions are expanded the UN inevitably will be asked, 'Do we help them leave or help them stay?' Which should have priority: assisting transit and reception of those who have been able to move or the prevention (if that is possible) of further exodus? In both cases the impartiality of the UN may be compromised. Recently, UNHCR field staff have been hampered, detained, abused. The agency has lost one life each week.

In the third place there is the UN goal of finding a lasting solution to homeless migration. There are evident links between protection and solution. The task of UNHCR in its first days was eased when there was a consensus that in half of Europe authoritarian regimes were persecuting many of their citizens and forcing them to risk death by fleeing westwards. A convergence of humanitarian traditions and political interests enabled resources to be channelled into relief operations which lifted out the 'unfree' and usefully imported brain and manpower into the booming West. It was never so in Africa. Both within UN circles and elsewhere there is vigorous discussion of the assertion that those who protect cannot escape looking at development – its approaches, its targets and its methods. The refugee has almost totally renounced any active role in decision making governing his or her own living conditions and is virtually dependent upon an authority over which he or she has no control. This is the grim reality of living in limbo. How is independence to be built? In the largest of terms, in what ways can the international community help, for instance, Africa to cope with the good years of plenty and the lean years of famine? Smaller-scale projects are being tried. In Cambodia and in Nicaragua one solution is now put to the test. A Quick Action Project is designed to bridge short-term relief (no solution) and development schemes. Counselled by team workers from UN specialised agencies (UNHCR, UNDP, FAO, WHO), a community chooses its own priorities, elects its own leaders, manages its own way of working. Foreign experts do not necessarily 'know best'. Income-generating activities underpin development. Development this way builds in prospects for lasting settlement, aids reconciliation among individuals and groups and affirms self-sufficiency.

Expecting the UN to find a final solution to dispossession is asking a great deal. Questions abound. How long is settlement likely to hold? The political dimension was very obvious in the Gulf area in 1991 and it led to three successive uprootings. As war clouds gathered thousands of Arab 'guest workers' left Iraq for Iran, Jordan, Syria and Turkey. Then, as Saddam Hussein moved to reassert postwar dictatorship ten times as many crossed into Iran. Later, as Baghdad turned upon its Kurdish minority in the northern mountains 60,000 Kurds panicked. UNICEF had to call in the help of allied airpower to underwrite 'Operation Provide Comfort'. Protection of refugees had turned into a military operation. What else could a relief agency do to offer protection? The name given the operation perhaps illustrates its limitations and those of UNHCR. Comfort is no real solution to anything. Another example of the cyclical nature of migration is the situation in the Horn of Africa. Here in 1995 there was a dance of death with 400,000 Sudanese deserting Ethiopian transit camps against a counter-flow of almost the same number of Ethiopians leaving

Somalian hutments. Neither governments in the region nor UN representatives were able to sort matters out.

Sometimes it looks as though a solution of some duration is in sight. In the summer of 1996 UNHCR made a determined attempt to peg things down in Western Sahara where conditions in the transit camps were deplorable. A contingent of 3,000 UN personnel, civilians and soldiers, set about careful counselling of the camps' inmates. The consequences of their choosing to return home to broken-down villages were explained followed by a ballot to see what proportion readily accepted the option of going back. Airlifts were organised to put down prospective settlers into carefully supervised and provided-for locations. It seems here and in the case of the Quick Action Projects that the essence of successful resettlement as a solution depends upon a democratic and informing programme. This goes beyond the expediency of adequate funds and competent managers which may clear the crowds clamouring for relief, but they do no good if the poor return to emptiness and humiliation leaving one dead-end to end up in another.

Finally, should not the newer approach to displacement be the forging of a really effective task force? Naturally, the progress made will always be conditional upon the consent and understanding of governments. It is already ten years since the bold unitary initiative of the UN's Organisation for Emergency Operations in Africa (OEOA) dispelled the notion that protective responsibility should be a sacred mandate held close to an independent heart. Rather than four specialised agencies blazing divergent paths, a coordinated rank of UNDP, UNHCR, WFP and UNDRO took on the broad functions of the Security Council on the ground – peacekeeping, peace-making, peacebuilding through a human rights watch, a rudimentary early warning system, contingency planning, resources deployment, first-aid relief, rehabilitation, economic revitalisation. It was an ambitious undertaking. Mistakes were made, valuable lessons about scope and approach and timing were learned. In its experimental way it was a move towards a more holistic view of what the migrant needs, deserves and, as the UN Charter affirms, has a right to.

TOWARDS THE FUTURE

The UN's effort to protect and revitalise the refugee can only bear fruit if it is approached realistically and optimistically. In the words of Bertolt Brecht, 'first we must eat, then comes morality'. There seem no real technical obstacles to prevent a concerted drive to redistribute resources to enable people to stand upon their own feet, securely and in dignity. Fifty years after the Charter's first pronouncements we still find wholehearted commitment of signatories insufficient. One recent suggestion gaining ground is that the UN should establish a Social Council as a principal UN organ in line with the Security Council. This body would supervise and integrate the work of all UN activities in relation to social (socio-economic) development and environmental protection. Working with the Security Council and an Economic Council and the General Assembly there would be fashioned a network of policy guidelines as an advance to sustainable development. Not all of this weighty recommendation finds favour in New York but it does point to a realisation that collective effort needs more vigour, authority and clarity.

Looking after the refugee is not only a prime concern of UN members: it is an essential part of civilised life. In June 1995 the High Commissioner for Refugees, Sadako Ogata, put it in these terms to a UN conference in Copenhagen: 'A multi-dimensional concept of peace must include not only freedom from war but also from want. Without that, people may come home, but for how long? And at what cost to the peace process itself?'

Part III

Facing the future

9 Prospects for UN internal reform

It is sometimes said in New York that the UN muddles through watched by 'uncritical lovers and unloving critics'. The UN at 50 is not short of critics nor, in many places, of rather complacent followers. As the millennium approaches the mood of reform is also to be caught inside the UN Building. The former Secretary-General, Dr Boutros Boutros-Ghali, has put in motion a fairly far-reaching restructuring of departments and staff, and he has sponsored a series of keen organisation and methods scrutinies. It has not helped that elements in the US Congress have been so virulent and generalising about UN personnel, financing, policies and programmes. Inevitably, some sections of UN opinion have taken the hostility hard, accusing Washington of a wrecking escapade and of blindness to what the UN has already done and can still do. Politics and press indulge in 'UN bashing'. The American eagle has become an ostrich.

The need for change is generally admitted in the UN. It will only come about if distorted images, ignorance and misrepresentation are met head on. Major reforms will almost certainly involve amending the Charter and member states, sincere about improvements, will have to be prepared for that. Minor reforms, financial and structural in the main, will still require consensus but can be drafted, debated and possibly accepted through enquiry, feasibility study and report.

Two things about reform are virtually certain. First, the major powers sitting comfortably in the privilege of the Security Council reveal marked reservations about any reform thought damaging to their status and interests. That applies to the mirror image of Washington as to everyone else. Second, from a wider perspective, UN reforms can only be rated as failing or succeeding if the attitudes of UN member states change.

This chapter will enumerate a number of aspects of this mammoth organisation which are widely thought worthy of review. Very much a selected list, it outlines some of the more obvious problems, enumerates recommendations from various quarters and goes on to stress some of the reservations that hinge on suggestions for internal change. Areas scrutinised will be, first, the institutional structures of the Security Council, the General Assembly and ECOSOC, and, second, important and controversial procedures to do with financing the UN, with peacekeeping, and with arms control. Readers are invited to speculate in what respects it might be possible to improve what the contemporary UN stands for. Criticism, after all, is meant to help. For T. S. Eliot it was 'strong black coffee'.

UN STRUCTURE: THE SECURITY COUNCIL

Problems

Anachronistic, it reflects the power constellations of 1945. Today its members represent one in twelve of UN members. Its permanent members are an exclusive clique. Too much goes on behind closed doors augmented by 'leaks'. A secretive cabal decides substantive matters which are then justified to the rest. The veto, originally a self-protective balancer for five major powers, is out of date and undemocratic. Coercive competence in peacekeeping, envisaged in the Charter, has been reduced to erratic persuasion, long vitiated by superpower clash and partisan role in complex regional disputes. The contemporary Security Council is weak and irresolute, lacking both pacific and forceful means of crisis and conflict management. Resolutions lack authority and decisiveness. International law arguments are not effectively used in liaison with the International Court of Justice.

Recommendations

- Membership should be enlarged from fifteen to twenty or twenty-five, possibly to include Germany, Japan, India, Brazil, Nigeria, Egypt and the EU. Useful criteria to decide this might be size, population, economic power, and perhaps military strength. There should be fair regional representation, for instance, from Europe, Africa, Asia and Latin America. Members must have equal status and equal access to all discussion.
- Permanent membership could be increased to ten. Alternatively, all members would be non-permanent, elected for two years.
- The veto needs to be replaced by majority voting.

- Regular consultation and working parties etc. with other states and 'interested parties' could usefully link the Security Council and the General Assembly. These meetings need not always be in New York.
- Dispute and conflict resolution have been tried with varying success over the years as peacekeeping modes. They need to be better coordinated and managed (see also the section on peacekeeping, below).
- Transmission of legal submissions from the Security Council through to active consideration by the International Court of Justice should be done more effectively.

Reservations

Reform of the Security Council means amending the Charter. Even one permanent member could block that with a veto. Opposition from the United States and the United Kingdom is set hard against radical reform and particularly against any loss of veto power.

The United States is fairly sure of retaining dominance, France is moderately confident, and the United Kingdom seems pessimistic and defensive. Admission of Germany and Japan would lead to stronger financial support. Would their character as economic giants from the North appeal to some struggling states in the South sensing decisions skewed to politico-economic ends?

Security Council membership would lead to more peacekeeping involvement. The attendant risk of association with any failure has to be balanced against the chances of success.

THE GENERAL ASSEMBLY

Problems

It is a place, in one US view, 'where noisy rhetoric, distorted priorities and vote trading appear beyond reform'. In some respects the General Assembly appears marginalised by a Security Council expanding into areas given over by the Charter to the General Assembly. Nevertheless, macro-economic issues, human rights violation, the use of tribunals, frontier readjustment, disputes are all quite legitimate areas for the Assembly, so why, it is asked, should the Assembly be accorded an inferior ranking?

Within the General Assembly a number of things are in need of reform. There is a constant and unsatisfied clamour from African and Asian nations for a reconstructed world economy and fairer distribution of world resources. International economic relations seem to them dominated by industrially advanced states.

An overloaded agenda has to be got through in three breathless autumn months. As for Decades and Years marking out the lines of proposed Assembly concern the one may be too long and the other too short for sustained implementation. Nor can this crucial sector of the world's international assembly be said to have any recognised legislative power.

Recommendations

- The General Assembly must reassert authority and competence in the areas of peace and security, humanitarian matters, human rights and arms control. The Assembly 'confers' primary responsibility for peace and security onto the Security Council; it cannot evade all responsibility. The Secretary-General reports directly to it. It elects two-thirds of the Security Council. It enjoys unlimited scope in debate and resolutions.
- Peacebuilding deserves a higher Assembly profile. Fact-finding missions, supervision of elections, and aid-in-transition need firmer support.
- Economic cooperation and development call for an Assembly regulatory and supervisory function beyond initiation of studies and reports. The IMF and the World Bank are not the sole institutions in this field of global concern and should assume a clearer partnership role – 'donors' partnering 'receivers' in the general work of the Assembly.
- Democratising the General Assembly necessitates a more systematic approach to building alliances with others. Wider representation gives opportunity for fresh realities, aspirations and suggestions. Reconstruction could establish two chambers, one for states' delegates, the other for national delegates elected by their own country, many of whom ought to be young delegates allowed proper access and participation.
- Closer work is desirable with regional and sub-regional organisations (like the OAS, OAU, the Islamic Conference, the Arab League, ASEAN, the Andean Pact, the EU).
- A small group of eminent, competent people (perhaps ex-heads of state, and experts) could feed in useful counsel from time to time.

- Continuous monitoring of General Assembly resolutions, statements and declarations is essential to establish priorities and check procedures and progress.
- Voting procedures are ripe for further review. Some system of weighted voting might ensure a fairer and more consistent share of Assembly work.
- The General Assembly could certainly work the whole year through with the aid of small, efficient working groups. The agenda needs to be shorter and better composed.
- The legislative possibilities of the General Assembly demand reconsideration and the Assembly should not be just a talk show. The legal affiliate of the Assembly, the International Law Commission established in 1947 to examine and codify legal issues and codify as much as possible, calls for reinvigoration.

Reservations

Persuading such keenly autonomous institutions as the IMF and the World Bank to collaborate closely with the General Assembly will be a hard task.

Only governments have authority to carry out the commitments the Assembly authorises. In what ways might wider representation create an authoritative voice and competence?

How far may NGOs and other 'unconventional' groups go beyond mere accreditation in 'joining' the UN without sacrificing something of their effectiveness, independence and diversity?

Voting reforms will trouble larger member states worried about losing some of their voting power. How important, though, is the voting? Should the General Assembly not be a centre for harmonising views and actions rather than a combative arena where differences are expressed, recorded and often magnified?

ECOSOC

Problems

ECOSOC is thought by many to be unwieldy with fifty-four states as members, six functional commissions, five regional commissions, six standing committees, and 600 affiliated NGOs. Eighteen specialised agencies report annually. Jealous of their autonomy, they are separate from the coordinating ECOSOC. Often their efforts are duplicated and some have not adapted well to new demands since their foundation in

1945. Planning at a distance between headquarters and field teams frequently leads to imprecise mandates and uneven results. In ECOSOC publications, survey reports and debates, basic social and economic conflicts well up and call for an integrated response. The crux of reform will be to persuade member nations to enact significant legislation and finance field programmes. Maintenance of peace and security does include the satisfaction of basic human needs as well as coping with violent conflict. Peacebuilding through preventive and development strategies has to have urgent attention. Developing states want the assistance of the IMF and the World Bank but see these as too much concerned with deregulation and financial easement, benefiting only the rich.

Recommendations

- A slimmer ECOSOC would improve direction and policy formation if it were able to use a central group of states' finance ministers who are action orientated. Subsidiary working groups would then have clearer agendas. Detailed programming would be done by task groups in touch all the time with host governments, experts and voluntary agencies.
- Development strategies to be effective are best implemented by the UNDP (already active in 150 countries). Priorities must include: strengthening in-country planning capabilities, eliminating long delays in recruiting consultants and field managers, kick-starting agreed projects, enlisting local management under host-country leadership, and the monitoring and audit of procedures and progress. Liaison with NGOs and voluntary bodies is desirable wherever possible.
- Specialised agencies might revert to their fundamental responsibility for information gathering, feasibility studies, programme design and specialist publication leaving the fieldworking to UNDP. That would help to rationalise and focus the talents and initiatives of thirty-six development agencies prone to duplicating efforts.
- Progress towards realising sustainable development is critical for all development policies. ECOSOC must mastermind guidelines for this.
- Regionally integrated projects linking several countries are feasible with careful interagency teamwork.
- Improving the UN's early warning of potential humanitarian crises demands more support from states for the new Department of

Humanitarian Affairs (DHA) to address natural and human disaster relief promptly. The DHA can deal with global economic problems more objectively than the IMF and World Bank. Aside from the financial advice and help of these institutions policy making must be in the hands also of representatives of developing countries.

Reservations

Thirty years ago the UN suggested that rich states offer 0.7 to 1.0 per cent of their gross national product as unconditional aid to the poorest states. Only four states (three Scandinavian) have managed this. (The UK and the USA hardly reach half of this proposed figure and often prefer conditional aid to more profitable projects.) Is 'donor fatigue' here to stay?

The World Bank has announced more emphasis and support for private capital sectors rather than putting up money of its own for prestige projects. Is this likely to bring in another move to aid-with-strings?

FINANCING THE UN

Problems

The UN relies on the goodwill of member states and their readiness to sponsor activities. Arrears, though, have accumulated with the United States and Russia the main debtors among seventy-eight others. Disagreement with some UN policies during the Reagan era of the 1980s has pushed US indebtedness to $1.4 billion (over half of the UN's regular budget of $2.4 billion). Successive presidents Bush and Clinton have had to wrestle with a Congress wanting to scale the US assessment down from 25 per cent to 20 per cent and to introduce weighted voting on budgetary matters. The original democratic premise of members' financial assessments being related to their capacity to pay induces some states to declare that while they 'pay most' their decisions may be voted down by those who 'pay least'. The use of voluntary methods of fundraising, for example for humanitarian work, leads to shortfalls, when funds arrive later than the beginning of the calendar year. Richer states may bring influence to bear. Some states, for instance developing states and Russia, suffer from low-income or economic transition difficulties and find regular payment of dues a problem. Washington's calls for a 'lean and efficient

UN', for 'doing more with less', seem unhelpful. Will the UN be able to put progressive improvements in hand if the cash flow is reduced to an unreliable trickle?

Recommendations

- Internal financial reforms to continue at the UN must be pressed in regard to budget ceilings, voting, allocation to priority programmes, costs of administration and staffing.
- Reform improvements before the UN at present: annual assessments to be paid in four instalments, peacekeeping to be financed by separate assessment, humanitarian and development costs to come from voluntary contributions. National defence budgets could be tapped legitimately to pay for some of these measures to enhance security. The United States and Russia and a number of other defaulters to make up arrears. A reappraisal of contributions from newly rich states in the Middle and Far East is due.
- For late payments penalties such as interest charges could be levied. Even so, states in very real economic and financial straits deserve tolerance.
- Alternative, even unorthodox, means of raising revenue are worth exploring. Costs might be shared with regional associations benefiting from peacekeepers' presence (NATO, OAU, OAS, ASEAN).
- Some levelling out of peacekeeping contributions could result by reducing US assessment from 31.7 per cent to 28.75 per cent or to 25 per cent (its payment to the UN general budget) and then picking up the difference from G7 members with high economic growth rates.
- Some development and peacekeeping operations merit closer examination not to abort them but to ensure finances are appropriate and steady. Peacekeeping costs are rising sharply and now touch $3.6 billion compared with the UN's regular budget total of $2.4 billion. This is where the greatest shortfall in members' contributions occurs.

Reservations

Heavy dependence on large payments from relatively few states makes the UN vulnerable to political pressures. Spread over 185 members the principles are democratic but actual levies need scrutiny from time to time to ensure their fairness. 'Slimming down' an organisation may save money but does not necessarily improve efficiency.

Relying on voluntary contributions especially from private sources carries a risk of conditional fund-giving or withdrawal if donors do not endorse UN policies. Raising money in this way would be neither easily predictable not controllable when it arrived.

The only assets and capital the UN has are the political commitment and goodwill of its members. Issuing threats to delinquent states to meet their arrears is unlikely to work. Long-term financial planning is not easy given the separateness of specialised agency budgets and in the case of peacekeeping its sporadic and widely varying characteristics.

PEACEKEEPING

Problems

Security Council resolutions give the UN impossible tasks, often concerned more with consequences than with causes. Really important decisions about peace and conflict are taken elsewhere making it difficult to decide and frame quick, appropriate responses. Traditional peacekeeping modes rely on neutral interposition, observation, etc. Recent missions (e.g. Cambodia, Somalia, Bosnia) have included a significant force component hazarding impartiality and risking miscalculation and impotence. Peace enforcement is difficult, possibly counter-productive. Initial fact-finding, preventive negotiation, use of sanctions, deployment of a task group, the extent of any force and follow-up rehabilitation frequently seem *ad hoc* decisions. Though situations and locales differ there is need for unambiguous guidelines especially where a UN force is exposed to fluid domestic politics. Good liaison between New York and field headquarters, between military and civilian elements, is vital.

The Military Staff Committee called for in the Charter does not function. An advisory and directing body is needed to work with the Secretary-General and the Security Council. The franchising of armed force by powerful states on behalf of the UN (as in Korea and in the Gulf) leads to difficulties over goodwill, objectives, modes employed, logistics, communications. Nor is there any standby force. The UN relies on members' undertaking voluntarily to assist peacekeeping.

The financing of peacekeeping is irregular and unassured. When a planned operation raises contentious issues the enterprise may be endangered because voluntary contributions as well as material support are withheld in disapproval.

Recommendations

- Peaceful methods of dealing with conflict in stages must be given priority, that is pre-conflict *preventive diplomacy*; pro-conflict *peacekeeping*; and post-conflict *peacebuilding*. (These approaches have been discussed in Chapter 4.)
- Intervention criteria need to be clearer since basic situations are not always a consequence of aggression, rather they may be the result of natural disasters, violence and gross human rights violation. Fast talking and concise agendas have to replace sporadic consultation and ill-defined mandates. The utmost care must be taken to avoid political 'interference' where a UN force is in contact with non-government and irregular parties. Teams of military and civilian experts could set up field headquarters as a preliminary relief and report centre within hours of any Security Council resolution which authorises intervention.
- The Military Staff Committee might be better constituted as a military planning unit or as an international military support staff unit. It would use state-of-the-art intelligence gathering and satellite surveillance to facilitate early warning and accurate ongoing data. This directive centre would be on constant watch with a 'surge capacity' should any crisis worsen.
- Standing force arrangements necessitate Charter amendment. States might agree to support a rapid response force of perhaps 100,000 volunteers on, say, five-year engagements. There could be a role for young volunteers here. Ideally, detachments of the force might be stationed in regional centres judged unstable. They would take a special oath of allegiance, procedures and equipment would be standardised, training unified and supplies usefully pre-positioned.
- Secretary-General leadership needs defining, assisted by a small team of deputies charged with specific responsibilities.
- Finance must be urgently and radically reviewed. UN members' contributions could be reassessed as a percentage of each nation's defence budget. Could not then the contribution rise if a state's arms spending went up and be lowered if defence expenditure was reduced? The peacekeeping bill has to be compared with the much greater cost of *not* undertaking peacekeeping. Reserve

funds need to be substantial with perhaps extra levies for complex and costly operations.

Reservations

Intervention as an issue is highly controversial. There may be reluctance to provide personnel, facilities and funding.

Controversies frequently erupt over aspects of particular operations as in Bosnia where force might be used in particular circumstances, or impartiality was thought in peril, or mandates were variously interpreted.

Nations supplying contingents to a UN force prefer their own command autonomy and ways of working. Raising and deploying any unified UN force can be difficult.

Pre-conflict preventive diplomacy is time intensive. Sanctions, and any form of embargo, certainly require forbearance if they are to take hold firmly and fairly. It is not easy to prevent parties to a dispute taking some other, perhaps irreversible, line of action.

ARMS CONTROL

Problems

The UN has not really made progress with disarmament as a total process but it has always been involved positively in various procedures for reduction, control and verification. Measures to effect arms limitation because it was difficult to resolve the issue of nuclear weapons have generally switched to addressing conventional armaments. Promotion of limitation and campaigns to alert people to the cost and dangers of the arms race have not been able to break down the barrier of states asserting their right to fortify. The Nuclear Non-proliferation Treaty has been extended indefinitely while deep resentment remains over permanent members' nuclear dominance and their apparent refusal to eliminate nuclear weapons as a long-term goal. Safeguards against covert nuclear arms production, stocking and trading remain dangerously loose. Efforts to attain a Comprehensive Test Ban Treaty over thirty-five years still encounter delay and sidestepping. Altogether the main progress in arms control has been achieved through lowered tension and confidence building measures chiefly in Europe, but other destabilised areas in Africa and the Middle East seem resistant to ordered control. Unfortunately, trading in weapons of many kinds continues with no discernible let-up.

General Assembly resolutions to curb this activity are met with states proclaiming their duty to assure their own defence (often in alliance).

Recommendations

- More progress internationally has been secured since 1987 than in the preceding forty years. This is mainly due to the greater accord between the superpowers when the UN has been an observer rather than a participant.
- Confidence building measures would go a long way to reduce tension and arms acquisition. Constant and wide-ranging monitoring of defence trends is inescapable as a means of enhancing confidence among nations.
- UN arms control needs to be more sharply focused on the limitation of specific types of weapons.
- Arms control could usefully be decentralised using control, surveillance and verification centres in unstable regions.
- What the IAEA has done to research and establish 'safeguards' for nuclear weapons seems a promising way of dealing with some other weapons.
- The UN should continue its advocacy of Nuclear Free Zones and No First Use agreements as barriers to nuclear proliferation. Disarmament Decades and Special Sessions, while not bringing conclusive agreement, have been impressive information exercises.
- The grey area distinguishing military uses of certain materials (nuclear, chemical, biological) and their civilian application needs further investigation and recording. 'Challenge inspections' can be profitable steps towards a mandatory verification regime.

Reservations

Furnishing security assurances to less powerful states has brought the UN little success.

Collaboration with regional (security) organisations is essential.

It is difficult to dislodge the confidence of 'peace-maintainers' who believe that nuclear capability in the hands of 'responsible' states deters potential peace-violators.

Verification by UN arms teams always comes up against the wall of national sovereignty exclusion. It is not easy to see how any General Assembly resolution can insist on site access and data on production and deployment if these are regarded as 'top secret'.

The UN encourages all states to avail themselves of access to nuclear 'know-how'. Will some developing states see enhanced military standing and energy improvement as inalienable rights? Are some control measures likely to increase dangers where states prohibited from 'going nuclear' arrange for large conventional forces or experiment with chemical and biological devices? Nuclear states with large weapon stocks are insisting upon warhead 'stockpile stewardship' policies to keep their weapons safe and reliable. This will be a difficult problem to solve.

A FINAL WORD

Radical reform of the UN is perhaps unlikely even if the majority of member states could agree on what sort of radical changes were desirable. Step-by-step modifications in some of the areas discussed above are more likely, indeed probable. With the five permanent members of the Security Council mainly in agreement on a range of issues the windows of opportunity are now less frosted over. Undoubtedly, a number of internal reforms will come about: the question is, in what form and when? And in what ways will such reforms not only reshape the UN itself but also bring about changes in the international environment? In what ways will the UN, reformed or unreformed, shape the future of international society? We shall consider this puzzling question in the following and final chapter.

10 The UN shapes the future

An evaluation

The critical question of how far UN members were able and willing to reform the Organisation was looked at in the last chapter. As the millennium approaches, will the UN be seen as sure of its mission, robustly able to face up to suggestions, even criticism? Poised at the dawn of the twenty-first century will the UN be regarded as a force able to bring about changes in the contemporary world? To draw up a balance sheet of UN performance is a complex and lengthy business. It is not easy to evaluate success and failure, since one person's choice of criteria might not suit another's. One way to deal with this problem is to summarise what previous chapters have described and questioned, to follow that with a brief selective list of some UN accomplishments in the fields this book has dealt with and then to return to the question of the UN as a force for change. This may help the reader attempt the task of appraisal individually or with others.

THE UN AS AN IDEAL

In 1945 the UN was created by fifty-one states with the immediate twin aims of guarding the peace and rehabilitating a battle-weary world. Long-term purposes, in the words of the UN Charter, were determination to save succeeding generations from war, to reaffirm faith in basic equal human rights, to establish respect for international law, and to promote social and economic progress. A General Assembly was to provide a forum where nations could discuss challenges and issues they were unable to cope with on their own. A Security Council would exercise a custodial watch over peace and security, empowered by consensus among five powerful states. Principles would be transformed into action by states functioning as an informed, purposeful and competent syndicate. Promotion of what was just and fair and humane would be the function of the UN as a kind of missionary centre.

THE UN BALANCE SHEET

A balance sheet, on the debit side, will show shortcomings. The grand vision of universal enterprise and the implementation of improvement has gone by fits and starts. The General Assembly, for instance, has split three ways, into Great Powers, secondary powers and non-aligned states. A majority of states have customarily retreated behind an exclusive shield of sovereignty and fortress defence. In the Security Council agreement in the early days was rare. Permanent members relied on the veto to protect particular interests. Self-determination expressed as an inalienable right frequently led to battles over colonialism. It has contributed also to minority contests within states which the UN finds hard to meet through mediation or intervention. Although Hot War on a grand scale has been avoided, instability throughout the world shows that peace is not conferred but has to be worked for. Peacekeeping by the UN has sought reconciliation in various ways and not always successfully. The UN mission to promote social and economic advancement in developing lands, planned on a mammoth scale, has inevitably met with political, ideological and cultural problems in the field. Progress overall has been fragmented. An account such as this does not make for comforting reading. Perhaps it does point to aspects of the work of the UN which its members themselves find unsatisfactory, even puzzling, given the mission statement of the UN Charter and the brave hopes of the UN's founders.

On the credit side of the balance sheet are the many things the UN has achieved, often in challenging circumstances and with the slimmest of resources granted by member states. Some of the achievements in the fields discussed in previous chapters are outlined below.

Infrastructural change

The UN has served as a forum for 185 states to discuss, consult, co-operate and formulate strategies to address global problems. Decolonisation, self-determination and independence have been promoted and the UN as midwife has brought over eighty formerly dependent territories into full UN membership as autonomous states. Transition programmes have helped many countries. Democratisation has been advanced through electoral counsel, assistance, supervision and help with constitution drafting in sixty countries.

Human rights

Basic human rights have been promoted and protected through definition in Declarations, Covenants and campaigns, the creation of monitoring and enquiry bodies and worldwide research, and teaching and training programmes. Refugees, 30 million of them, fleeing from persecution and war since 1945 have been protected and assisted. Migrants seeking asylum have been helped by the UN actively encouraging states to fashion reception and resettlement schemes.

Peacekeeping

The UN has painstakingly developed means of conflict resolution in stages through preventive diplomacy, preventive deployment and peacebuilding. Thirty-six peacekeeping operations have been launched with varying mandates and varying success but only three of these initiatives have had to employ enforcement.

Arms control and disarmament

The UN set up the International Atomic Energy Agency (IAEA) in Vienna in 1957 to monitor and control the peaceful or illicit use of nuclear energy. Nuclear proliferation has been addressed through the Non-proliferation Treaty, 1968, which is reviewed every five years. The Treaty now bans weapons proliferation indefinitely. Prohibition of nuclear weaponry has been secured for a number of these areas – Antarctica, 1959, outer space, 1967, Latin America (Tlatelolco) Treaty, 1964, the sea bed, 1972 and the South Pacific (Rarotonga) Treaty, 1985. Nuclear testing has been limited by the Partial Test Ban Treaty, 1962, the Threshold Test Ban Treaty, 1974, and the Peaceful Nuclear Explosions Treaty, 1976. A Comprehensive Test Ban Treaty has been in draft since late 1996. Agreements have been secured to limit biological weapons in 1972 and 1992. A Chemical Weapons Convention (CWC) was ratified in 1996.

A Committee on Disarmament was set up in 1984 to take over from bodies formed in 1946. The wider task of providing facilities for all member states to join in discussion and the need to raise public awareness of the complex issues in disarmament and arms control have been the purpose of Special Sessions on Disarmament organised in 1978, 1982 and 1988.

Economic and social affairs

ECOSOC was established to coordinate a network of eighteen specialised agencies, commissions, committees and task groups with the general responsibility for ongoing and emergency relief, funding, technical support, education, training, and negotiation of trading agreements. In 1944 the World Bank (IBRD) was set up by the Bretton Woods Conference to help raise loan capital for poorer states, to facilitate investment there, and generally to maintain a balance of payments equilibrium wherever it was possible. At the same time the International Monetary Fund (IMF) was instituted to work for balanced trade and stable currencies. Three years later the UN founded the General Agreement on Tariffs and Trade (GATT). There are now something like ninety-seven subscribing states (some 97 per cent of the world's trade).

Development

The UN's spearhead for this sector of activity is the UN Development Programme (UNDP) set up to coordinate 6,000 development schemes in 150 countries. There is a stress on long-term five-year country and intercountry schemes. Africa has been given special attention latterly with a massive UN Programme for African Economic Recovery and Development in 1986 and in 1996 a ten-year UN System-wide Social Initiative on Africa with $25 billion for concrete action plans. Two aspects of development planning and implementation are being given increasing prominence: urbanisation and sustainability. The first addresses the burning problems associated with rapid town growth – population pressure, economic and social patterns, rejuvenation of run-down and undeveloped hinterlands, and local management projects. Second, sustainability in the face of environmental degradation has high and urgent priority. The UN convened world conferences in Stockholm in 1972 and in Rio de Janeiro in 1992 to rally forces for a collective drive to save a fast-vanishing planet. Development is now to be 'eco-friendly', carefully managed and controlled only by international consensus. Constant 'Earthwatch' surveillance systems monitor trends, needs and progress. Conventions on climate and biodiversity were agreed at Rio in 1992.

Summits

Some of the more important world conferences for states' delegates and NGOs to decide about global issues have been organised under the auspices of the UN. The process has developed rapidly in the aftermath of the Cold War and includes such important conferences as: Children 1990 New York; Environment 1992 Rio; Human Rights 1994 Vienna; Social Development 1995 Copenhagen; Population and Development 1995 Cairo; Women 1996 Beijing; Human Settlements 1996 Istanbul. In this respect, the UN is seen to provide a neutral focus and forum for international debate and recommendation.

The UN as an agent of change

We ought now to return to the original question: can the UN be regarded as a force able to bring about changes in the contemporary world? In its fiftieth year is the UN merely a forum for state action or is it in reality an independent actor or is it both of these? Theoretically, and in accordance with the Charter, the UN enables member states to demonstrate their adherence to the principles of that Charter. The General Assembly and Security Council in different ways facilitate meeting, consensus and decision. That this has come about at all and that it is still in place is testimony to a widespread recognition that concord and shared enterprise have in many cases displaced and must continue to displace anarchic individualism. In practice, of course, the UN is a melting pot where feelings of complementarity of interests, purposes and needs are vaguely and variously interpreted. Member states are diverse in their political and ideological orientations, in the roles they feel called upon to play, and in their historical and contemporary experiences. Coming to the UN Building in New York are representatives of democracies, autocratic regimes, revolutionaries, would-be liberators, religious fundamentalists, the poor and the proud. The grand assembly of nations lasts three months each year but at other times decisions are made within committee rooms and corridors. Given this diversity and the sporadic nature of encounter can the UN in any real sense be described as an actor?

The principal responsibility of the Secretary-General and of committee leaders is to work towards agreement and the consequent framing of resolutions and guidelines as a precursor to actions which the UN's action components are then authorised to carry out. These components are the Security Council (the UN's executive arm) and the specialised agencies, which, as we have noted earlier, work more or less as a network. Perhaps it is most helpful to think of the UN not so much as an actor but as a *regime*.

A regime may be defined as a set of mutual expectations, rules, regulations, norms, explicit principles, organised energies and financial commitments which have been accepted by a group of states. It is both structure and process. For the participants in the regime, expectations about particular issues will converge. There will be trust that commitments are openly and loyally declared and reasonably and reliably fulfilled. Decision is the prevailing practice. The bringing about of change for the better in external circumstances will certainly be a motivating force for any regime while success in doing this serves to justify the principles endorsed by the regime. It is unlikely that any regime will feel entirely certain at any one time that full success is being achieved but at least this helps to give encouragement and purpose to the members. In the case of the UN, it could be said that if its members do not agree on preferred outcomes to their actions then at least they generally agree as to the outcomes they wish to avoid. The alternative to conflict, in this instance, is peace and progress by all possible means.

If, therefore, we think of the UN as a regime and in that sense as a possible initiator of change, there are at least two clear ways in which, as embodiment of structure and process, it has both changed itself and mirrored changes in the world at large. First, in regard to structure, the pluralistic regime of 1945 depended on a core of hegemonies (stabilising master powers), five in number, the pillars of the Security Council. Their prestige and power to move ensured that change was to be the preserve of the strong, standing in a common UN front. Eventually, two of the hegemonies, Britain and its Commonwealth and the Soviet Union, were to undergo a decline in power and status compared with 1945. France, it can be argued, has always been something of a junior partner, while another, the United States, has found its intentions and drive blunted by others unhappy over the consequences of unilateral action. The American veto was increasingly resorted to as a result from the 1960s. The one permanent member of the Security Council to have definitely *increased* its power is the People's Republic of China. Ignored in the 1940s, its agreement is essential to international consensus today. Meanwhile, both at the UN and in the world outside there has been a growth of interaction and fluidity among smaller units. The original reliance on benevolent hegemonies has given way to the realistic perception that the contemporary world is interdependent and multivariate in national characteristics, perceptions and needs. From the 1960s into the 1990s, change has tended to stem from non-alignment, which disdains allegiance to a common front. Yet, notwithstanding changes in global international relations, particularly in respect of transnational interdependence and the diffusion of power, there has remained at the heart of the UN a good deal of 'preservationist' fervour. As J. S. Nye has recently pointed out, the UN is still a 'layer cake' of stratified, institutional power with little sign of it crumbling or being eaten away by external forces. The permanent powers stoutly resist any modification of their ascendancy. *Plus ça change. . . .*

The regime of the UN has changed rather more in regard to process. For three decades after its birth in 1945 the UN had to watch impotently the matching of raw power constellations as the superpowers held the ring with their associates with peace depending on a sensitive Balance of Terror. The gradual easing away from impasse through *détente* to tentative trade-offs was mainly brought about by bilateral negotiation. With the end of the Cold War, UN members have begun collectively to address crisis and conflict at regional and national level. Examples of a 'peace process' steered by members of a much less quarrelsome Security Council have demonstrated that action by an international organisation can attempt to foster change in such different situations as Bosnia, the Gulf, the Middle East and Rwanda. However, what is equally apparent is that the process of change, or rather its likelihood, still seems to depend upon the prime movers, the common front of certain major powers. They have the say-so that governs the possibility of action by the UN's Security Council.

Evaluation in most dictionaries has the quantitative element of ascertaining value (or amount) and the qualitative element of estimating worth or merit. This is an individual matter for both people and states. Any judgement can be seen as idiosyncratic. In this sense, the UN's 185 members are well aware that they are trying, often in uncertain and clumsy ways, to shape the future not only of an international organisation but also of their contemporary world. In general terms they endorse what President J. F. Kennedy knew the UN to be, that is, 'our last, best chance for peace'. As they look out from the UN Building at a changing and exploding contemporary world, many members must recall a forthright verdict on the success of the UN, a verdict intoned on numerous occasions. It is: 'the UN has not been tried and found wanting – it has never really been tried'. Should that not be understood as an obligation for member states to try again – and to try harder?

Guide to further reading

BOOKS

Baehr, P. R. and Gordenker, L. (1984) *The United Nations: Reality and Ideal*, New York: Praeger Publications. Rather pedestrian in style and outlook.

Bailey, S. D. (1989) *The United Nations: a Short Political Guide*, 2nd edn, London: Macmillan. Deserves its accolade as 'a marvel of compression'.

Balassa, B. (1985) *Change and Challenge in the World Economy*, New York: St Martin's Press. Not an easy read but shrewd analysis.

Barrs, D. (1992) *The United Nations Kit*, Cambridge: Pearson Publications. Imaginative kit for schools' use.

Berridge, G. R. (1991) *Return to the UN*, London: Macmillan. Thoughtful discussion.

Bourantonis, D. and Wiener, J. (eds) (1993) *The United Nations and the Quest for Nuclear Disarmament*, Aldershot: Dartmouth Press. Competently put case.

—— (1995) *The United Nations in the New World Order*, New York: St Martin's Press. Informative essays, some over-wordy ones. Good notes.

Davies, P. (ed.) (1988) *Human Rights*, London: Routledge. Well-balanced essays. No index.

Evans, G. (1993) *Cooperating for Peace*, London: Allen & Unwin. Keenly analytical. Strongly recommended.

Falk, R. A., Kim, S. S. and Mendlovitz, S. H. (eds) (1991) *The United Nations and a Just World Order*, Oxford and Boulder: Westview Press. Forty-one authoritative essays. Useful bibliography but no index.

Ferguson, J. (1988) *Not Them but Us: In Praise of the United Nations*, East Wittering, West Sussex: Gooday. Concise, well presented.

Gordenker, L. (1987) *Refugees in International Politics*, London: Routledge. Very useful account.

Gordon, W. (1994) *The United Nations at the Crossroads*, New York: M. E. Sharpe. Wide view, up to date. A US perspective.

Gregg, R. W. (1993) *About Face: the United States and the United Nations*, Boulder and London: Lynne Rienner. A vigorous US argument.

Hurrell, A. and Kingsbury, B. (eds) (1992) *The International Problem of the Environment*, Oxford: Oxford University Press. Comprehensive, thoughtful.

James, A. (1990) *Peacekeeping in International Politics*, London: Macmillan. Excellent source. Good on detail and history.

Jensen, E. and Fisher, J. (1990) *The United Kingdom, the United Nations*, London: Macmillan. Descriptive studies. Slow moving in parts. Useful index, bibliography.

Kegley, C. W. and Wittkopf, W. H. (eds) (1985) *The Nuclear Reader – Strategy, Weapons, War*, New York: St Martin's Press. Highly readable discussion.

Leontief, W. W. (1977) *The Future of the World Economy: a UN Study*, Oxford: Oxford University Press. Dated but factually sound.

Luard, E. (1982, 1989) *A History of the United Nations*, Vol. 1 (1945–55) and Vol. 2 (1955–65), London: Macmillan. Very readable.

—— (1994) *The United Nations: How it Works and What it Does*, London: Macmillan, 2nd edn. Slim but poses keen questions.

Moynihan, P. (1980) *A Dangerous Place*, New York: Berkely Books. Frank writing by US Ambassador to UN in 1970s. Regarded by many as virulent and unhelpful criticism.

Osmanczyk, E. J. (1990) *Encyclopaedia of the United Nations and International Relations*, London: Taylor & Francis. Indispensable reference work.

Peterson, M. J. (1986) *The General Assembly in World Politics*, Boston: Allen & Unwin. Straightforward examination.

Pitt, D. and Weiss, T. G. (eds) (1986) *The Nature of United Nations Bureaucracies*, London: Croom Helm. Ten essays, thoughtful but some laboured. Poor index.

Riggs, R. E. and Plano, J. C. (1995) *The United Nations: International Organisation and World Politics*, 2nd edn, Chicago: Dorsey Press. Well organised. Useful notes and suggestions for reading.

Roberts, A. and Kingsbury, B. (eds) (1993) *United Nations, Divided World*, Oxford: Clarendon Press. Carefully edited essays. Useful appendices, excellent index. Up to date.

Steele, D. (1987) *The Reform of the United Nations*, London: Croom Helm. Easy to read and cross-refer but rather inconclusive.

United Nations (1985) *The United Nations and Disarmament 1945–85*, New York: United Nations. Sound historical account. UN information sources (see below) can provide updated information in this field.

—— (1990) *The Blue Helmets: A Review of United Nations Peacekeeping*, New York: United Nations. First-rate reference source. Regularly updated.

Urquhart, B. (1987) *A Life in Peace and War*, London: Weidenfeld & Nicolson. Direct experiences of an old UN 'hand'. Invigorating.

Whittaker, D. J. (1989) *Fighter for Peace. Philip Noel-Baker 1889–1993*, York: Sessions. Biography of League of Nations and UN founding figure. Useful references.

—— (1995) *United Nations in Action*, London: UCL Press. Complements this book with series of case studies especially for students. Useful references.

World Commission on Environment and Development (1987) *Our Common Future* (Brundtland Report), Oxford and New York: OUP. A mine of information and critical analysis.

And in most public and college libraries:

Keesing's Record of World Events (formerly, *Keesing's Contemporary Archives*), London: Longman. Easy-to-use reference source monitoring world information sources. Updated supplements each month.

JOURNALS

From time to time articles about the UN and its work appear here:

Foreign Affairs International Affairs International Organisation International Relations International Studies Millennium Review of International Studies Political Science Quarterly The World Today Third World Quarterly

USEFUL ADDRESSES

Full information on all aspects of UN involvement worldwide may be obtained from these sources:

United Nations Department of Public Information
Promotion and Public Services Division
Public Enquiries Unit
UN Plaza
New York
NY 10017
USA
Tel: 001212-963-9245

United Nations Information Centre
Millbank Tower (21st floor)
21–24 Millbank
London
SW1P 4QH
Tel: 0171-630-1981

United Nations Information Service
UN Office at Geneva
Palais des Nations
1211 Geneva 10
Switzerland
Tel: 004122-917-1234

United Nations Sales Section
Room DC2-0853
New York
NY 10017
USA
Tel: 001212-963-8302

United Nations Association – UK
3 Whitehall Court
London
SW1A 2EL
Tel: 0171-930-2931

United Nations Association – USA
485 Fifth Avenue
New York
NY 10017
USA
Tel: 001212-687-3232

The UN Chronicle (from the UN Department of Public Information) is published quarterly on a modest subscription basis. Very useful.

UN special agencies provide a wealth of material free and for sale. Their addresses can be got from the UN information sources listed above.

Index